Archaeology

Archaeology
A Concise Introduction

Alice Beck Kehoe
University of Wisconsin-Milwaukee

Thomas C. Pleger
University of Wisconsin Colleges
UW-Fox Valley and UW-Baraboo/Sauk County

Long Grove, Illinois

For information about this book, contact:
Waveland Press, Inc.
4180 IL Route 83, Suite 101
Long Grove, IL 60047-9580
(847) 634-0081
info@waveland.com
www.waveland.com

Cover photo: Dr. James Stoltman photographing 1992 UW-Madison excavations of a stratified multicomponent Woodland site near Prairie du Chien, Wisconsin. Photo: Thomas Pleger.
Frontispiece: Chaco Canyon, Pueblo Bonito doors. Photo: Thomas Pleger.

10-digit ISBN 1-57766-450-7
13-digit ISBN 978-1-57766-450-5

Printed in the United States of America

7 6 5 4 3 2 1

Contents

Preface

Archaeology, the science of the human past, is now also a business employing thousands. Students should know something of our past and how it is studied. They should know, too, that they can earn a living as an archaeologist or participate in research as a volunteer. Beyond the practical benefit to interested people, students as citizens should understand that remains from the past are our heritage, our patrimony, to be protected for generations to come. Because archaeology involves all of us as taxpayers and property owners, teachers need resources to include archaeology in college anthropology and secondary school social studies courses. We prepared this book to be useful and readable, sound but not ponderous.

Tom Curtin, anthropology editor at Waveland Press, proposed such a book to the senior author, Alice Kehoe. She agreed to write it as a collaboration with a younger archaeologist, someone more directly involved with the latest technology and Cultural Resource Management (CRM) regulations. Tom Pleger was the person she had in mind, a younger man who is an excellent scholar and field researcher, sincerely concerned with undergraduate education and public outreach. We have both enjoyed this collaboration and believe our complementary experiences, woman and man, older and younger, Plains and Woodland, give our book good balance.

First and foremost, this book is the result of our years teaching introductory anthropology and archaeology. The book is short enough to fit into a general introductory anthropology course and solid enough to be a backbone text for introductory archaeology courses. We know that students have probably watched *Raiders of the Lost Ark* or *Lara Croft, Tomb Raider*. They've heard of Egyptian mummies and King Tut. They may have a photo of Stonehenge as desktop screen on their computer. We tell them about famous sites, about pseudoscientific claims and myths about archaeological finds, and along the way we explicate basic scientific method. We draw attention to the growing global business of heritage tourism and the archaeological goal of stewardship, preserving the patrimony rather than digging for goodies. With our own autobiographies illustrating the sweep of experiences available to anyone—neither of us comes from a wealthy or socially prominent family—we help students become aware of the past in the present, a segment of the economy, and opportunities to participate in its pursuit.

The book is organized logically from an opening description of the field of archaeology as discipline and profession, and a brief history of its development. Chapter 2 explains how an archaeologist conducts research, with particular emphasis on contemporary practices in North America. To keep things interesting, we highlight the "Romance of Archaeology," featuring sites so famous that cartoonists do riffs on them; we debunk nonsense while pointing out how much more intriguing the historical facts are. Then we illustrate actual careers in archaeology with our own autobiographies; Alice's is longer than Tom's because she was already launched into fieldwork when he was just a kid. Chapter 6 introduces "Controversies That Never Die"—brainless zombie science, we call them—and leads us into explaining scientific principles, critical thinking, and serious debates over enduring questions. We conclude with a chapter on heritage management and an overview of the sweep of archaeology.

We both believe that our complementary, although overlapping, experiences strengthen the book. By avoiding the impersonal, we hope we can draw instructors and readers into linking their own experiences into the picture. We want to make it clear that archaeology is a part of everyone's life.

Alice Kehoe
Milwaukee, Wisconsin
Thomas C. Pleger
Menasha, Wisconsin

Chapter One

What Is Archaeology?

Archaeology! Mummies with golden masks! Fearless explorers at the Temple of Doom! Mystery! Romance! "When I was a kid, I wanted to be an archaeologist, but then I had to make a living . . . ."

These are lines we hear over and over. Real archaeology offers much more. Real archaeology connects with everyone, nearly every day. Around us lies our patrimony from the past—what we inherit from all our ancestors, the lands they made habitable, and millions of fragments from their lives. Federal and local laws protect our patrimony, and thousands of archaeologists earn their living by identifying it and working to preserve our heritage for the future while accommodating contemporary needs. We'll tell you how, and why.

Archaeology is a science at the edge where science meets the humanities: archaeology's methods are scientific while it draws upon the humanities to interpret its data. Everyday archaeology can be pretty routine, requiring patience, care, and enough people skills to get along with fellow crew members, bosses, landowners, and casual visitors. Behind the routine are intellectual challenges, both the puzzle-solving kind and those of theoretical argumentation. Puzzle lovers can take on the task of fitting together fragments to make a picture of ancient life—a jigsaw puzzle with most of the pieces lost. Serious thinkers can debate about human nature, the nature of human societies, and human development—from primitive ancestors living off the land to contemporary society with its global technology webs. Archaeologists run the gamut from family-next-door wage earners to prima donna professors pontificating on world trends. If you'd like to be an archaeologist, it's actually a sensible occupational choice—and if you don't think you'd be happy as an archaeologist, you still should know something about our vast past, the foundation of all our societies today.

WHAT DOES THE ARCHAEOLOGIST DO?

Once upon a time (it was 1889), a young couple carried their infant son in a basket to their archaeological excavation project. He grew up to combine many years of fieldwork with deep reflection upon the practice of history and philosophy of knowledge. Out of this unusual melding of experience as field archaeologist and as professor of philosophy, R. G. Collingwood wrote of the real, true past-in-itself—infinite, every breath of every thing that ever lived, every wind and wave and crumbling sand grain—and our *known* pasts, drawn from ruins and old documents and from our assumptions that people used to live and think more or less as we do. Professor Collingwood emphasized that we ask questions about the remnants of the past that we find, and frame a known past out of answers we discern in these data. The real, infinitely vast past is more than we can ever comprehend, and the bits of data preserved from the past do not speak directly to us. Archaeologists *construct* pictures of little sections of the human past out of data they manage to recover. As scientists, we archaeologists take pains to record accurately both what we find—and, at least as important, its context—in the ground and in relation to the society that created it. What we try to avoid—as a later archaeologist remarked when lecturing on Collingwood's distinction between the real, infinite past and known pasts—is the tendency to concoct a "wished-for past," colored by our dreams of what might have been.

As scientists, archaeologists examine what remains from human activities in the past. Note that we deal only with *human* activities—no dinosaurs, no natural rocks. We look for evidence of *activities*; if we encounter human bones, we bring in biological anthropologists to work with them. We survey landscapes, looking for landforms (such as mounds) resulting from human activities, and for preserved human-made objects such as stone knives and broken pottery sherds. We use electronic imaging tools (see the next chapter) to reveal buried evidence such as wall remnants and hearths, and we test the imaging by digging. Once surface sod has been stripped off, that digging is carried on with sharpened mason's trowels, shaving off dirt without harming or dislodging what may remain. Where no evidence of past activities is visible on the surface or by high-tech imaging, but a location would be suited to human habitation and is threatened with destruction, we sample with shovel probes every-so-many meters. If nothing of human activity is found, we conclude that the developer can go ahead, although there are many instances where big earthmoving equipment uncovers sites that the archaeological consultant could not observe (whereupon the developer may be asked to halt until the archaeological material is removed or analyzed in place). Archaeology today is basically a business protecting our patrimony from uninformed obliteration.

WHAT ABOUT THOSE TOMBS AND TEMPLES?

Archaeology began as a scientific discipline along with other natural sciences in the early modern period, the seventeenth century in Europe. People in many areas of the world, including Europe, had been interested in ruins and artifacts—things made—from former times, but generally did not systematically study them. They were often attributed to supernatural beings or legendary rulers. During the Renaissance in Europe, around the fifteenth century, new appreciation of literary, architectural, and artistic productions from Classical Greece and Rome, one thousand to nearly two thousand years earlier, spurred careful descriptions and scholarly comparisons.

Many wealthy persons collected beautiful antiquities and paid laborers to uncover more, a hobby that came to be called "antiquarian pursuits." Antiquarians assumed finds would agree with Classical texts, which led the nineteenth-century businessman Heinrich Schliemann to explore the area in Turkey that contains many Classical Greek ruins, and settle upon one site as the city of Troy described in Homer's *Iliad*. Walter Scott, the Scottish historical novelist (who wrote *Ivanhoe* and *Rob Roy*), titled one of his books *The Antiquary*. The title character buys an estate and tells visitors that an embankment in a field is part of the border wall built by the Roman general Antonius. One day an old man stops to say that as a youth, he and other lads built that bank for the previous owner's agricultural improvements. The antiquary is greatly upset that he can no longer boast of a Roman ruin on his property.

Antiquarian researches, focusing on beautiful ancient objects and tying them to classical texts, also flourished intermittently in China and in Peru around AD 1400, at which time the Chimu kingdom artisans copied pottery made 1500 years earlier. With the founding of the Royal Society of London in 1660 and similar aristocrats' scientific clubs in other countries, including the American Philosophical Society in Philadelphia in 1743, a different approach to archaeological material slowly developed. Instead of beginning with a revered text, the Bible or centuries-old classical writings, these intellectuals advocated hands-on observation of phenomena and logical inference about their functions and causes. If phenomena were in places outside Classical civilizations around the Mediterranean or Biblical lands, then logically there would not be any texts with which to place them in context. Scientists began to look at peasant folklore and customs, and at non-Western peoples for clues to understand prehistoric finds.

The word *prehistory* was first used in English by the Scottish archaeologist Daniel Wilson in an 1851 book classifying collections of antiquities in his country, and then in his landmark 1862 book, *Prehistoric Man*. Between the two books, Wilson had emigrated to Canada and spent summers canoeing on Lake Superior with Ojibwe (Anishinaabe) Indians, learning to respect their technology and knowledge. Wilson's book sold out its three editions quickly, but a competing book by the rich Londoner Sir John Lubbock became better known as Lubbock's friends in the Royal Society cited it rather than its rival by Wilson. Lubbock, with no field experience in archaeology or ethnography (his own research was on an ant farm in his mansion), maintained the English boast of superiority over conquered countries, terming native peoples of the Americas "savages."

America's national scientific research institution, the Smithsonian, strongly supported archaeological and related anthropological studies. Its first publication, in 1848, was *Ancient Monuments of the Mississippi Valley* by Ephraim Squier (who later explored ruins in Peru) and Ohio medical doctor Edwin Davis. The two men painstakingly mapped the enormous earthworks of the Ohio as well as central Mississippi valleys, revealing to the world Hopewell, the prehistoric remains of an American Indian culture that built mounds and embankments in the shapes of immense geometric figures—an entire golf course lies inside one circle, at Newark, Ohio. We now know that Hopewell is nearly two thousand years old. After the Civil War, veteran Major John Wesley Powell launched both the Geological Survey and its sister, the Bureau of American Ethnology, within the Smithsonian. Powell's admirably diverse staff, including several women and educated American Indians, recorded indigenous languages and cultures and the distributions across the continent of ceramic, stone artifact, basketry, and fabric types. By the beginning of the twentieth century, the American Museum in New York, the Peabody Museum of Harvard University, the Field Museum in Chicago, the Milwaukee Public Museum, the University of California at Berkeley, and other institutions were amassing collections from both prehistoric and contemporary American First Nations, publishing descriptions and producing educational exhibits for the public.

In the twentieth century, universities took over the role museums had played in encouraging archaeology. Undergraduate and graduate

A map of the huge, two-thousand-year-old geometric earthworks of Hopewell in southern Ohio. Note that the ancient circles and rectangles are as big as city blocks in the town of Chillicothe (center). From Ephraim G. Squier and Edwin H. Davis (1848), *Ancient Monuments of the Mississippi Valley*.
—*Inset:* This falcon effigy, made of native copper from the region of Lake Superior, shows Hopewell metalworking technology. It was placed in a tomb that included other copper artifacts and pearl- and shell-bead necklaces, all covered with sheets of mica. Photo: Courtesy of National Park Service, Hopewell National Historical Park.

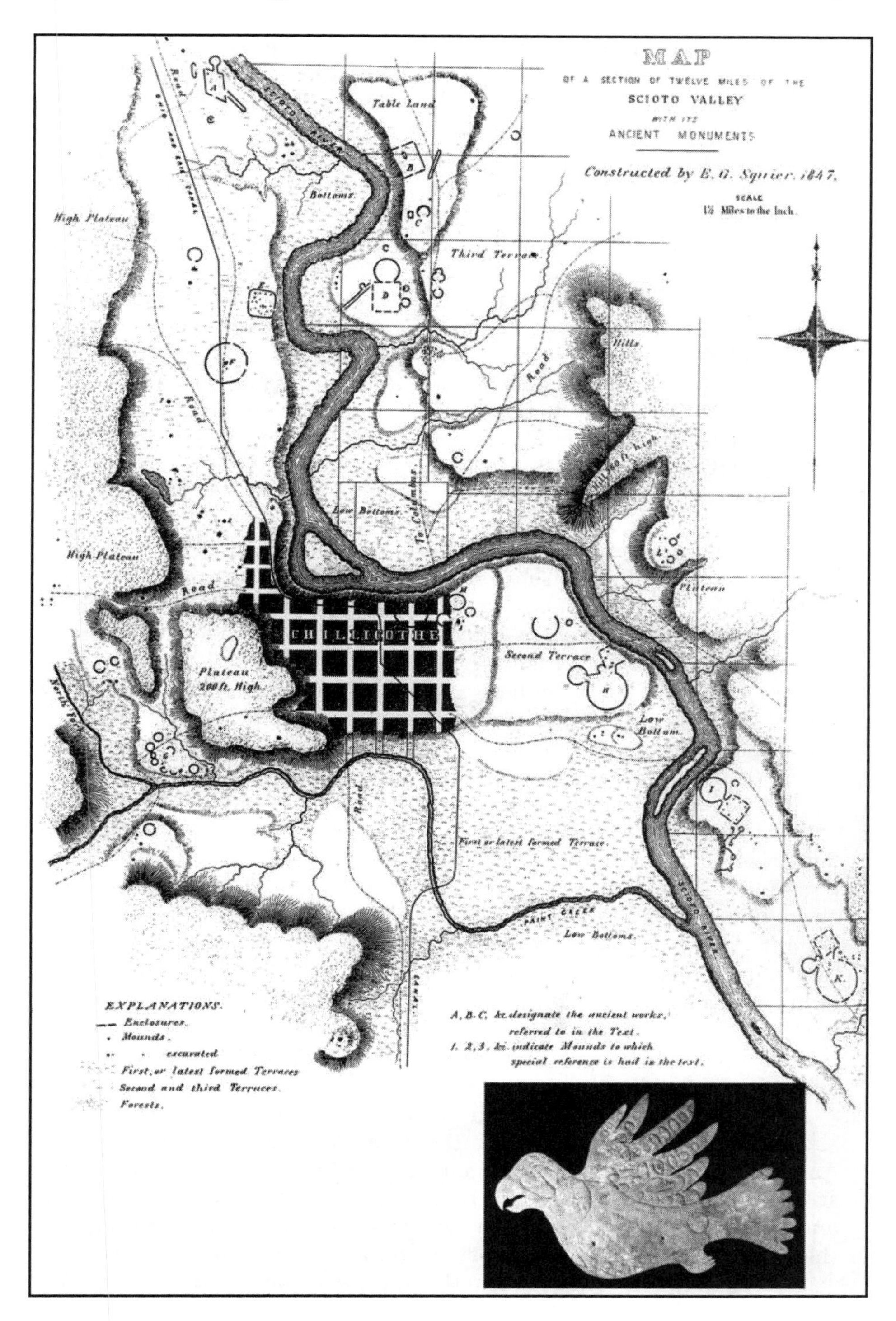
MAP
OF A SECTION OF TWELVE MILES OF THE
SCIOTO VALLEY
WITH 172
ANCIENT MONUMENTS
Constructed by E. G. Squier. 1847.
SCALE
1½ Miles to the Inch.
Table Land
Scioto River
Bottoms.
High Plateau
Third Terrace.
Hills
Road
Low Bottoms.
To Columbus
High Plateau
CHILLICOTHE
Plateau
Second Terrace
Plateau 200 ft. High.
Low Bottom.
First or latest formed Terrace.
Paint Creek
Low Bottoms.
North Fork
EXPLANATIONS.
Enclosures.
Mounds.
excavated
First, or latest formed Terraces
Second and third Terraces.
Forests.
A, B, C, &c. designate the ancient works, referred to in the Text.
1, 2, 3, &c. indicate Mounds to which special reference is had in the text.

degree programs were established, leading to the expectation that archaeologists would be formally trained and credentialed. During the Great Depression of the 1930s, relief projects for laborers were frequently archaeological excavations, because numbers of unemployed people could be engaged in archaeology with very little expense in terms of tools or facilities. Proliferation of these projects required organization to ensure that the excavations were conducted scientifically and that the finds and records were curated and results published. Some states systematically surveyed their patrimonies, stimulating conferences to compare data over larger regions as well as to monitor projects. In 1935, the national Society for American Archaeology (SAA) was founded to promote professional standards for archaeology, reach out to serious amateurs, and publish a scientific journal, *American Antiquity*. SAA continues to serve as the Americas' primary archaeological organization, its annual meetings being *the* place to hear and be heard about archaeology.

Colleges and universities expanded after World War II, in response to the huge increase in students due to the G.I. Bill offering veterans financial support for post-secondary education. This boom in post-war higher education fostered introduction of anthropology and archaeology courses. Protests against authority and conformity in the 1960s drew many students to learn more about cultural diversity. The G.I. Bill, the 1964 Civil Rights Act, the affirmative action initiative, and the rapid growth of "minority" populations all solidified the realization that living in today's world demands broad knowledge of human ways. Questions about the history and nature of human diversity intrigued the thousands of students who would enroll in archaeology classes. Their professors during the 1950s, 1960s, and 1970s carried out projects designed to illuminate these questions. Much of this "problem-oriented" research was funded by the National Science Foundation, under its mandate to improve public understanding of science (to strengthen America in its Cold War competition with the Soviet Union). Ambitious younger archaeologists saw that the more "scientific" their project proposals looked, the more likely they were to get grants and jobs. Led by Lewis Binford, they announced they were practicing a "New Archaeology" that was "explicitly scientific," which tended to mean they used a lot of statistics and focused on quantitative analysis over qualitative or descriptive data.

Meanwhile, decades-long efforts to protect America's patrimonies succeeded in establishing, first, the 1906 Act for the Protection of Antiquities, then the 1966 National Historic Preservation Act and the stronger 1974 Archeological and Historic Preservation Act. With states and municipalities enacting their own laws to spell out and supplement the federal decrees, ignorant destruction as well as looting for profit was forbidden. To comply with the laws, the business of cultural resource management (CRM) grew rapidly after 1974, by the 1990s employing thousands of archaeologists. A Master's degree in anthropology with archaeological training has been sufficient for most CRM jobs, shifting the focus in the profession from academic problem-oriented projects (and careers) to surveys, testing, and salvage excavations, with results written up in reports for enforcement regulators rather than for scientific journals. A great number of CRM projects simply report "nothing found," letting planned construction proceed. Regardless of whether or not significant heritage is identified, the CRM archaeologists get paid for their work. CRM has contributed greatly to our understanding of the past, because considerably more archaeology has been carried out under cultural resource management requirements than in earlier years, and much of it in localities that would not have been surveyed or tested without these mandates.

Tombs and temples, today, are likely to be preserved with minimum disturbance. *Stewardship* is the theme: our responsibility is to be stewards, maintaining what is left of the past for future generations to see and perhaps research. Museums are already full of beautiful objects taken in the nineteenth and early twentieth centuries, when sponsors expected crates of goodies pulled out of ruins. These are cycled around from city to city in special exhibits, while archaeologists may be back in the storage rooms analyzing trays of sherds, chopped animal bones, scraps of cloth, and other dull daily-life data passed over in the era of competition for the spectacular. Tourism makes many archaeological sites into destinations and brings in archaeologists to reveal more of historic structures and places. Thousands of people—kids, families, retired people—participate in professionally supervised archaeological work during vacations or as a hobby. (The U.S. Forest Service's "Passport in Time" offers many such opportunities.) It is, and isn't, romantic: One senses, as the trowel scrapes along a blackened hearth or stops at a flint flake, that one is in direct contact with someone from hundreds or thousands of years ago. As the day gets hotter and the soil bakes harder and you put another little scrap of deer bone into your level bag, romance may evaporate. Most of us archaeologists stay in the game because we do like being outdoors and handling real things, and when we stop for a moment to think about what we're doing, we are a little bit excited to realize we have discovered something hidden for many generations.

Talking Points

- Compare and contrast "science" and "humanities." Archaeology is a *science* because it limits its analyses to phenomena discoverable in the physical world, it measures and describes in precise terms, and it presents its data for public examination and discussion. It partakes of the *humanities* in that it seeks to recover human history; its phenomena include art, literature, and musical instruments insofar as they may be preserved; and it is concerned to evaluate the roles of religion, ideology, politics, world-views, and language in the societies of the past it investigates.

- Today we realize that interpretation of data is influenced by a person's *standpoint*. Is the archaeologist American, Canadian, Mexican, French, Chinese? Man, or woman? Upper class, bourgeois, or working class? Feminist, gay/lesbian, Mormon, Fundamentalist? Schooling differs by nationality, experiences vary by social class and gender, commitment to a particular doctrine colors what is accepted as valid. For example, Daniel Wilson, growing up as a poor Scottish boy, developed a standpoint to appreciate craftwork and living off the land, while Sir John Lubbock's standpoint of wealth and social privilege led him to see hunter-gatherers as brutish savages.
- Why is it important to conserve and protect our patrimony from the past? Antiquities laws in the United States apply primarily to public lands, whereas in many other countries, such as Canada, *all* relics from the past legally belong to the nation. Should the United States have domain over all antiquities, including those on private property? Is it the job of the federal government to protect archaeological sites, or is it also the responsibility of state and local governments to work together to protect our past?

Note

[1] Piggot, Stuart (1981), Summary and Conclusions. In *Towards a History of Archaeology*, edited by Glyn Daniel, pp. 186–189. London, Thames and Hudson, p. 187: "[T]he English philosopher-archaeologist R. G. Collingwood . . . [wrote of] an unattainable past-in-itself and a series of pasts-as-known. . . . To this several of us have . . . added a third past, the past-as-wished-for . . . we owe this felicitous phrase to Glyn Daniel, who first used it in an informal public lecture in the late 1950s."

Chapter Two

Tools of the Trade

As we discussed in the previous chapter, for the most part archaeologists study extinct cultures. How do archaeologists study societies that are no longer observable? There are, of course, multiple ways to study the past. For example, one can use oral or written creation stories to learn about a culture's past. Archaeology, by contrast, focuses on the residues left behind by ancient cultures. Archaeologists collect evidence left behind by ancient cultures to reconstruct ancient lifeways. We accomplish this by using scientific methods of data recovery, dating, and interpretation.

The *scientific method* of investigation attempts to maximize the potential for obtaining truth by using controlled and recognized methods that minimize bias and error. One of the hallmarks of science is that investigation must be based upon *empirical data*. Data is just another term for information, facts, or clues. "Empirical" means that the information or data must be observable, measurable, and real. Although this may seem fairly simplistic, it is important to realize that scientific archaeology can focus only on those aspects of the past in which we can collect real data to support or refute an interpretation.

For archaeologists, our data are taken primarily from material culture. *Material culture* refers to aspects of a culture that are manufactured or produced. We think about a particular culture in terms of two major components. First are all the behavioral aspects of the culture that reflect how people interact with one another—including the language, religion, kinship, and social organization. But behavior is only part of a culture. Culture also includes technology, and all of the things that humans produce or use in their daily lives. Think about your own culture in terms of religion, ideology, family structure, language; then think about all of the human-made items that are part of your culture: your clothing, your house, your automobile, your furniture, your appliances, and so on. These human-made objects are all examples of material culture.

Archaeologists study ancient material culture, or artifacts, to reconstruct or learn about the other aspects of culture that are less tangible. The term *artifact* is synonymous with material culture. An artifact is anything that is manufactured by a human being or one of our ancestors. Note that this definition means that artifacts do not necessarily have to be ancient; your pencil/pen, notebook, laptop and clothing are all artifacts. Think about the artifacts that we just mentioned and imagine how many of them might survive being buried for a hundred years, a thousand years, or even ten thousand years in your local environment. One of the problems archaeologists face is that much of the data (material culture) we study is perishable. Therefore, most archaeological sites contain only a small fraction of the items that once existed when the site was inhabited.

Material culture can be broken down into two subcategories. Generally, the term artifact is reserved for something manufactured by humans (or our ancestors) that is portable in scale. For example, imagine a room filled with furniture. Many of the objects in the room are artifacts—chairs, framed pictures on the wall, couches, tables—these are all portable. However, the room itself and the building in which it is located were both produced by humans and are forms of material culture. Technically, such immobile human constructions are artifacts, too, but archaeologists use the term *feature* to refer to artifacts that are not portable or that can only be removed by destroying the supporting material. Another example of a feature in the above scenario would be a fireplace within the room. The fireplace is human made, but it cannot be removed without dismantling part of the room and house. Prehistoric archaeological examples of features include houses, fire pits, trash pits, burial pits, burial or other human-made mounds, temples, and artwork drawn or carved into a cave wall. All of these items are human-made and are not portable. Archaeologists study the relationships between artifacts and features on an archaeological site to reconstruct extinct cultures.

In addition to artifacts and features, types of non-human-made data are also collected and analyzed. The term *ecofact* refers to objects that are the product of biological processes. Ecofacts are usually plant or animal remains that have not been modified by humans. Ecofacts can provide information about ancient environments and human diets. *Geofacts* are objects that are produced by geological processes. Geofacts are useful for interpreting site geology and land formation processes.

SITES

An archaeological *site* is a place where there are artifacts and/or features. Note that there has to be material culture present for a location to be an archaeological site. We are often asked how archaeological sites are discovered. In most cases, they are found by laypeople who are out on the landscape either for recreational reasons or because of their job. In northern Wisconsin, farmers, hunters, hikers, scuba divers, and avocational archaeologists regularly visit Tom's office with artifacts that they have found. One of the first questions he asks is: "Where were these artifacts found?" Information becomes useful to the archaeologist when artifacts have a known provenience or provenance. The *provenience* is the location in which the artifacts were found, both horizontally and vertically, in the ground or underwater.

Recording the location of artifacts at a site can easily be accomplished by using high-quality maps. Archaeologists often record site locations by using legal Township and Range descriptions, in which the site location can be narrowed down to a fairly precise subdivision of a quarter-section of land. Additionally, global positioning satellite (GPS) coordinates are now being used more frequently for locating sites. GPS works by relaying signals from satellites to a point on the landscape. Once the horizontal location has been recorded, we often ask whether the artifacts were found on the surface or if they were deeply buried and brought to light via construction or earthmoving.

Archaeological sites are also discovered as a result of professional surveys. Archaeologists use a variety of methods to detect sites within a given area. Pedestrian observation is the most common technique used all over the world. This is simply walking exposed soils along shorelines, plowed fields, construction areas, or other exposed surfaces looking for artifacts. Once artifacts are encountered, their location is mapped and the site's boundaries are determined. This works only for areas where one can see what is on the surface or in cuts. For areas that are covered with vegetation, whether it be a mowed lawn or dense rain forest, remote sensing methods must be employed.

Remote sensing methods are used when the researcher cannot see the targeted surface. There are two basic categories of this type of survey: aerial and subsurface. Aerial survey involves the use of high vantage points, aircraft, or satellite imagery. These types of surveys are looking for differential signatures on the surface of the earth that may be the result of underlying archaeological deposits. One method is to look for differential vegetation growth. Vegetation tends to grow more lushly where there are rich organic soils and often where people have left debris.

For example, in the mid-1990s Tom was involved in a project in southwest Wisconsin, where archaeologists were trying to relocate a series of burial mounds that were mapped in the late 1800s. After their mapping, the mounds were subsequently plowed down for decades as farmers used the land to plant their crops. When we arrived, there was no longer any visible relief attributable to the mounds—the fields appeared flat. However, when we climbed the neighboring bluff tops some 250 feet above the river valley, we could see circles of dense green corn in the middle of the farm fields. These circles coincided with the late 1800s mapped locations where the mounds once stood. The reason the corn was greener and taller in these areas was that the mounds likely contained burials in subfloor wooden tombs, enriching the soil as they decayed. Archaeologists similarly use aerial photography to locate archaeological sites that might not be visible on the ground. Satellites are also now employed to locate archaeological sites using infrared technology. Soil densities give off different infrared signatures, and human-made features tend to show up as defined areas of either hotter or cooler zones.

Subsurface remote sensing methods include a variety of techniques. The simplest is shovel testing. *Shovel testing* involves digging test holes on a grid at standardized intervals. The earth is dug by hand and all of the soil is passed through a screen, in which artifacts are then recovered. Test holes that produce positive results are plotted on a map. High-tech subsurface survey methods include ground-penetrating radar, resistivity, and similar electronic methods. These devices work by passing an electronic signal through the ground. The signal either passes through or reflects off different densities of materials in the soil. Ground penetrating radar devices are similar to electronic fish finders; they read soil anomalies by sending a signal down into the soil. A resistivity detector works by passing electrical current between vertical probes placed along a grid; it also documents anomalies in soil density. Unfortunately, these methods do not tell what is buried

Clockwise from top left:

—Stratigraphy. Archaeologist Thomas Kehoe twelve feet down, using his trowel to excavate the lowest, oldest layer in a series of bison drives. Note the butchered bison bones protruding from an occupation layer, middle left. Each little white tag marks a distinct layer, either soil or occupation. Dark layers were formed during more humid climate periods. Photo: Alice Kehoe.

—Kids can work as volunteers on archaeological projects. Here, two boys clean and sort butchered bone from the French Paleolithic site of Solutré. Photo: Alice Kehoe.

—Recording the pattern of remains in a bison drive. Archaeological assistant Alfred Heavy Runner (a Blackfoot Indian whose ancestors probably slaughtered these bison) draws each bone to scale, revealing the pattern of processing the kill. Photo: Alice Kehoe.

—Teresa Pleger shovel testing a site in Green Bay, Wisconsin. Photo: Thomas Pleger.

—UW Colleges students excavating Late Woodland habitation layer at the Chautauqua Grounds Site, Runnoe Park, UW-Marinette campus, Marinette, Wisconsin. Photo: Thomas Pleger.

—UW-Fox Valley student processing artifacts from excavations at the Chautauqua Grounds Site, Marinette, Wisconsin. Photo: Thomas Pleger.

beneath the surface; they only inform the researcher that there is something of interest there. The reading usually has to be confirmed via excavation in order to determine its significance.

Today, archaeological site inventories in most of the United States are maintained via geographic information system (GIS) computer databases. GIS allows archaeologists to store multiple data sets. For example, GIS site inventories usually contain sets of information on site location in terms of horizontal location and elevation, cultural affiliation, nearness to bodies of water, site size, site condition, ownership status, and other categories. By merging all of this information, archaeologists can search site inventories for particular site attributes. This allows a researcher to observe site patterns that previously, without the use of computers, would have been very difficult to isolate. GIS can also be used for predicting where certain types of archaeological sites might be found in relation to environmental features. This is particularly useful for estimating the impact of a proposed construction project such as a highway, dam, or other large earthmoving civil engineering project.

Once a site is discovered, archaeologists often test the site to determine its significance, size, and cultural affiliation. This is usually accomplished by establishing a grid over the site. The grid is basically a north-south, east-west, and depth-measurement system. The grid is tied into a datum point that is fixed to the landscape. This allows the archaeologist to select certain areas of the site for test excavation and to record the provenience of archaeological data recovered. Provenience refers to the three-dimensional location of an artifact or feature. Today, we use a transit or a total-base-station to set up the grid systems. Total-base-stations are optical transits that can receive and transmit GPS signals. Measurements are taken and stored in memory in the unit, from which they can later be downloaded to a computer to make accurate maps of the site.

Archaeological sites are considered either single-component or multi-component. Single-component sites have only one episode of cultural occupation. Multi-component sites are those that have been utilized for more than one period of time. Multi-component sites are more complex, as the archaeologist needs to keep the data from each occupation separate. This is one reason a grid system is used; it allows for the recovery of artifacts or clues so that their precise location can be documented. Understanding the stratigraphy of a site is critical to assessing the relationship of archaeological deposits that are from different time periods.

EXCAVATION

Stratigraphy refers to the study and interpretation of the layering of the earth. Generally, as one digs deeper into the earth, one moves back through time. The general rule is that strata or layers that are deeper are older than those above. Strata can be natural or cultural (human made). The job of the archaeologist is to discern how the strata were formed and to interpret the significance of each layer in relation to the archaeological deposits. Stratigraphy can also be used to assess the relative age of an artifact, feature, or deposit in relation to materials discovered in strata above or below.

The primary goal of an excavation is to reveal patterns about the past that can be used to interpret a particular culture. In order to do this, the archaeologist must decipher the context of the archaeological data. *Context* refers to an assessment of the quality of the data in terms of how it got there. There are two major types of context: primary and secondary. *Primary context* refers to archaeological materials that were deposited by the people who produced or used them. For example, imagine a group of prehistoric hunters killing a mammoth with a stone-tipped spear. The hunters then butchered the carcass and left the bones and stone tools in place after they consumed the meat. The site was subsequently covered by windblown sediments. Twelve thousand years later, an archaeological excavation uncovers the site. The excavation reveals a stone spear point embedded in the skeleton of an extinct mammoth along with a series of stone butchering tools and cut marks on the bones. The association of the mammoth bone and the stone tools would be considered to be in primary context. The artifacts (the stone spear point and butchering tools) and the ecofacts (the mammoth bones) are associated. *Association* refers to the fact that they were found together. Their association could be used to infer that the stone artifacts were used to kill and butcher the animal. Artifacts that are in primary context are of the greatest use to archaeologists because they can be used to interpret what activities took place at a site.

Secondary contexts are less useful because the deposit has been disturbed either by nature or by later cultures. Imagine the same scenario above, with the projectile point stuck in the skeleton of a mammoth and a series of stone butchering tools buried below the surface. Now image a farmer plowing the site to a depth that brings the bones and the artifacts to the surface of a field, and in plowing the spear point becomes separated from the bone. Although an archaeological survey may have located both the mammoth bones and the stone tools in the field, they are now in secondary context. The artifacts are in secondary context because their association with the mammoth remains can no longer be confirmed, and it is unclear how the artifacts got there. A similar situation could occur if the site had been severely eroded by torrential rains and/or floodwaters. If the water moved or transported the artifacts and the bones, the materials would now be in secondary context.

Archaeologists go to great lengths to record the context and associations of all data found in the field. This is very similar to what a crime scene detective does. The detective photographs, maps, and recovers all of the evidence so that the context of the associations of the clues can be understood. The same is true for archaeology: we want to preserve as much information as possible about the context and association of each find. Hence, everything is mapped, photographed, bagged, and labeled in the field so that provenience can be maintained even when the materials are back in the laboratory.

Generally, the excavation process is slow and methodical in order to be precise. Disturbed overburden soils can sometimes be removed via heavy machinery or via shoveling. Once hand excavation begins, sediments are removed slowly in layers, using shovels. Usually, all soils from the excavation are screened for artifacts. This is accomplished by sifting the soil through ¼-inch or smaller screens. When features or other deposits are discovered that could contain preserved ecofacts such as plant or animal remains, the soils may be excavated and bagged for flotation recovery. Flotation involves passing the soils through a device that uses water to "float" preserved organic materials to the surface. These are skimmed off with cheesecloth or some other filter fabric and then analyzed under the microscope for identification. The heavier artifacts sink to the bottom, where they are recovered in a screen trap.

As artifacts and features are discovered in primary context, excavators usually switch to hand trowels. The preferred tool is a sharpened mason's trowel. Trowels may be used in conjunction with small picks and brushes for very detailed excavation. The goal is to remove the sediments so as to reveal patterns that can be used to interpret what activities took place at the site. Once a pattern or group of artifacts and/or features is uncovered, it is usually mapped and photographed in both plan and profile views. The profile views show the stratigraphy in the excavation's walls and are important in understanding the relative age of each deposit.

When the artifacts and other field data are back in the laboratory, they need to be cleaned, sorted, counted, weighed, and catalogued. Then the analysis phase of the project begins. Generally, most archaeologists estimate that for every hour of field excavation there are an additional three hours of laboratory processing and analysis associated with the excavation.

Many artifacts are made of perishable materials (hide, wood, bone, plant fiber, shell, etc.), and therefore it is often necessary to stabilize an artifact to prevent further decomposition. For example, artifacts that are recovered from wet or submerged contexts often start to crack or split when they dry out. To counteract this, it may be necessary to slowly replace the moisture with a hardener. Besides this, many artifact classes need to be handled with care and stored in archival containers in order to avoid chemical contamination that may result in degradation of the material.

After the cleaning and preservation are done, artifacts are usually sorted by provenience and then further sorted by raw material, style, or manufacturing method. Once this has been accomplished, archaeologists can begin to search for patterns within the site. For example, certain clusters of associated tool types may lead to the understanding of how the site was used and by how many people over what period or periods of time. Computers are regularly used in this process to tabulate and sort data. Computers can be used to generate two-dimensional and three-dimensional maps of the site showing patterns or clusters of artifacts and features. GIS mapping can be applied across a region when looking at the distribution of archaeological sites, and it can also be applied at the site level to look at the distributions of artifacts and features across the site or between sites.

DATING

Archaeologists use a variety of methods to date archaeological deposits and sites. They either directly date an artifact or feature or date a deposit indirectly by dating something associated with it. Dating materials by association relies on a firm understanding of their context. Dating methods can be divided into relative and absolute dating techniques. *Relative dating methods* allow the researcher to compare the relative age between the items being dated. In other words, these dating methods are used to determine if artifact A is older, younger or the same age as artifact B. These dating methods do not produce an absolute date, only a relative date in relation to what the artifact is being compared to.

There are several types of relative dating. Stratigraphy is often used as a relative dating technique. By recording the stratigraphic position of artifacts and features at a site, archaeologists can date these deposits in relation to one another based on their vertical positioning in the ground. In order to use stratigraphic dating, archaeologists must make certain that their excavation methods maintain vertical provenience information for all artifacts and features.

Another relative dating method is *seriation*. Seriation works by comparing a series of styles or artifacts that were used over a period of time. Artifact types are grouped into series based on either their stylistic similarities or their frequency of occurrence. With stylistic seriation, the researcher arranges artifacts in a linear fashion based on technological or stylistic similarities. The resulting arrangement represents the evolution of a particular artifact's style over time. Imagine having a sample of automobiles from over 50 years of time. You could arrange the automobiles in a series representing time by comparing materials, body shape, trim, and other features. Although this method would not tell you how old each car is, it would allow you to infer which cars are older or newer than others. The same methodology could be applied to a series of stone projectile points, clay pots, or prehistoric house forms.

The second type of seriation is frequency seriation. This method is based on the premise that an artifact style will appear most frequently during the time it was used. Imagine excavating a deeply stratified archaeological site. Within the excavation, the archaeologist recovered four major stone projectile point types. The types may actually occur in all levels of the stratigraphic deposit, but there appear to be certain levels or strata that contain greater numbers of each point type. By mapping out the frequency of each point type in relation to depth, the archaeologist can determine the relative age of each particular point type. Again, this method only gives a relative age of the point types in relation to each other; it does not allow the archaeologist to know exactly how old any of the point types are.

Other relative dating methods are based on association. If artifact styles are found with extinct animal or plant remains that are from the last Ice Age, then the archaeologist would argue that the artifacts also date to the last Ice Age. However, the exact or absolute age of the artifacts is still unknown.

Absolute dating methods produce results that can be used to measure how old something is in relation to our own calendar system. There are a number of methods used by archaeologists. In historical archaeology, archived documents including property titles, newspapers, drawings, and photographs can provide dates for buildings, ships, and landscape changes. Prehistoric sites require collaboration with specialists from other sciences. Three of the most commonly used absolute dating methods are: dendrochronology, radiocarbon dating, and potassium argon dating.

Dendrochronology basically means tree-ring dating. Most people understand that a cross-section or core from a tree trunk can be used to determine the age of the tree. Each ring represents an annual growth period. The thickness of the growth ring is related to precipitation and varies each year. A tree-ring core is actually a fingerprint of the weather patterns at a particular location for a particular period of time. These signature patterns can be linked to ancient wood by identifying overlapping ring patterns. Using this method, tree-ring chronologies have been developed for long-lived species of trees. By creating a tree-ring chronology of a particular tree species in a particular area, archaeologists can use archaeological wood samples of the same species to date a site or occupation at a site. This is done by comparing the tree-ring growth pattern of the archaeological sample to the master chronology for the species. In some areas of the world, tree-ring chronologies extend as far back as 8000–9000 years ago. The major problem with this dating method is that it can only be applied to certain species of wood in certain areas of the world.

In the late 1940s, *radiocarbon dating* was developed at the University of Chicago. This technique is perhaps the best known by the public but many people do not understand the process. Radiocarbon dating works by measuring how much ^{14}C (the radioactive isotope of carbon) has decayed in relation to ^{12}C (the stable isotope of carbon) in ancient organic materials. All living things absorb ^{14}C and ^{12}C. The proportion of ^{14}C to ^{12}C remains constant in an organism during its lifetime. However, the ^{14}C is continuously breaking down in the organism's body because it is radioactive. When the organism dies, ^{14}C is no longer being absorbed and the amount of ^{14}C continues to decay at a constant rate without replenishment. Radiocarbon dates are based on measuring how much ^{14}C has decayed in relation to the amount of ^{12}C left in the sample. The half-life (the amount of time it takes for the material to break down to half of its original amount) of radiocarbon is 5730 years. This means that every 5730 years there will be half of the previous amount left.

To illustrate this, take a sheet of paper and fold it in half (this would be the amount of ^{14}C left in 5730 years), then in half again (this would represent the amount of ^{14}C left in 11,460 years), then in half again (this would represent the amount of ^{14}C left in 17,190 years). Eventually, if you keep folding the paper in half, you will reach a point where you cannot mechanically fold it any more. A similar situation exists with radiocarbon in that after approximately 50,000 years, standard radiocarbon dating methods can no longer measure the little amount left in the sample. Because of this, standard radiocarbon dating is useful only for materials that are less than approximately 50,000 years old.

Accelerator mass spectrometry (AMS) radiocarbon dating is a newer method that requires a much smaller sample. This method allows archaeologists to date materials that previously could not be dated because of their small size. AMS works well for dating textiles, wood fragments, hide, bark, and other preserved organics. AMS also allows for dating materials farther back in time and can extend radiocarbon dating to as far back as 100,000 years.

Radiocarbon dates are reported as a probability. The date is also calculated by subtracting radiocarbon years from AD 1950. Nineteen-fifty was chosen as an arbitrary point from which to measure elapsed time, because radiocarbon dating was developed in the late 1940s. A standard radiocarbon date of 5500+/–150 years BP (before present—measured from AD 1950) means that there is a 67% probability that the date falls between 5350 and 5650 years BP. AMS dates tend to have a greater probability and a tighter standard deviation than standard dates.

Scientists specializing in radiocarbon dating have been able to date tree samples from known dendrochronological dates. This process has resulted in the realization that the amount of ^{14}C in the atmosphere has not been constant over time, and radiocarbon dates of ancient wood samples older than 1500 BC tend to be too young. By comparing ^{14}C dates with dendrochronologies from several areas of the world, researchers have developed a calibration curve for radiocarbon dates. Dates that have been calibrated usually are identified in the report along with references to the particular calibration program that was used.

Potassium-argon dating is also a radiometric absolute dating method. It is similar to radiocarbon dating in that it is based on the measuring of ^{40}K, a potassium isotope. This particular isotope of potassium is radioactive, and as it breaks down it turns into ^{40}Ar, argon gas. The half-life of ^{40}K is 1.31 billion years old. It can be used to date deposits as recently as 100,000 years. This method is useful for dating when volcanic geological deposits were formed. Therefore, this method is used to date associated geological strata that contain, overlay, or underlie archaeological or fossil deposits. This method has been used extensively in Africa to date early pre-human sites.

Archaeologists often employ multiple dating techniques to determine the true age of a deposit. For example, stratigraphy may be used in conjunction with radiocarbon dating and seriation. The combination of these techniques increases the strength of the argument for a particular age estimate of the archaeological materials in question. There are a variety of other dating methods: obsidian-hydration dating, fission-track dating, uranium-series dating, and archaeomagnetism are just a few. Students interested in learning about these dating methods should consult an archaeological methods text such as Renfrew and Bahn's *Archaeology* (Thames and Hudson; look for latest edition).[1]

UNDERWATER ARCHAEOLOGY

"Nautical," "maritime," or "underwater" archaeology is carried out mainly on shipwrecks but can apply to buildings and living sites presently under water. Underwater archaeologists must be qualified divers to work safely, and they usually need support from a boat. The field is complicated by treasure hunters systematically searching for wrecks of ships, such as the galleons that set sail for Spain in the sixteenth century with cargoes of plundered Mexican gold. It is costly to outfit a ship and divers, so governments tend to allow privately financed salvagers to work so long as they record the finds, allow professional analyses, and donate an agreed-upon portion of recoveries to a public repository such as a museum. (Most accessible shipwrecks are not far offshore and therefore are within national boundaries.)

Reading a manual[2] on underwater archaeology can be amusing, seeing conventional tools such as surveyors' theodolites attended by masked floating figures. It isn't funny to archaeologist divers who struggle to remain in place against a current, mindful that their time underwater is limited. Recording exact provenience is as necessary underwater as on land, but how to write? Archaeologists use pencils or Magic Markers on Mylar film sheets attached to clipboards. How is a grid constructed? With colored low-stretch synthetic rope such as ski rope, marked at measured intervals with black tape and anchored with stakes (much stronger than those needed on land) driven into the seafloor or lakebed. Remote-sensing devices adapted for water, such as SONAR, are used to find promising areas for probing. Instead of scraping off soil with a sharpened trowel, underwater archaeologists frequently use an air-suction apparatus that pulls particles of mud up a tube and ejects them through a pipe onto the boat or shore. Archaeologists gently feed the loosened mud into the suction tube by fanning it with their hand off the buried artifacts or shipwreck. When an artifact or ship's timber is exposed and recorded with the same precision required on land, it can be removed for laboratory analysis and eventual curation, again demanding even more caution and care than most land projects need, for waterlogged materials deteriorate amazingly quickly when exposed to air.

Underwater archaeology is a serious and specialized field. Properly carried out, excavation of a site under water reveals a great deal about seafaring and inland waterway technology and cultures. States and Canadian provinces regulate care and investigation of their underwater archaeological resources, often with a designated full-time qualified staff. Students and adults certified for scuba diving may be hired or may volunteer for supervised underwater archaeology projects.

***

Archaeology is a scientific way of learning about the past. It uses a variety of well-established and recognized methods for site location, recovery of artifacts, and the dating of archaeological deposits. Archaeology is a particularly exciting field, not only because new data are constantly being discovered, but also because new methods of analyzing archaeological materials are being developed.

Talking Points

- Why are archaeologists so exceedingly fussy about precise measurements and exacting detailed recording of contexts? One answer is to remember that the archaeologist is a crime-scene investigator (CSI) minus the crime: the same care with which the CSI determines the way the crime was carried out and the character of the perpetrator also enables the archaeologist to understand the scene in past lives. Try thinking of your home as a site: Details of the context make all the difference (e.g., when it's you as a young teen walking in the door at 4:30 in the afternoon versus coming in at 1:30 in the wee hours!).

- Why do archaeologists use remote-sensing equipment, instead of just digging in likely spots? Part of the answer is to *find* likely spots, which may be buried under a foot or more of soil and not apparent to the naked eye. Equally important is that using remote sensing lets the archaeologist map out the general features and area of a site (subject to verification by limited shovel testing) without destroying it with complete excavation. This consideration is an aspect of the stewardship ethic so critical to archaeology today.

Notes

[1] *Archaeology: Theories, Methods, and Practice*, by Colin Renfrew and Paul Bahn, is a comprehensive, reliable, and easy-to-use resource covering all aspects of archaeology. Editions are regularly updated.

[2] We recommend Jeremy Green's *Maritime Archaeology: A Technical Handbook*, published by Elsevier Academic Press in 2004 (2nd ed.). On a more popular level, George F. Bass's *Beneath the Seven Seas: Adventures with the Institute of Nautical Archaeology* (Thames and Hudson, 2005) vividly describes dozens of famous and fascinating underwater archaeology projects.

Chapter Three

Exciting Archaeology

Technology can be fascinating, but there's a lot more to archaeology than standard procedures and high-tech devices. There are spectacular sites, and most of them still have ongoing archaeological investigations. We'll show you some famous ones here.

KING TUT AND THE PYRAMIDS

Ah, the Boy King—why did he die so young? Murder? And the Curse of the Pharaohs upon the archaeologists opening his tomb! Any time Ancient Egypt is mentioned, we almost automatically envision the golden mask of the youthful pharaoh's mummy. Sometimes we see the exquisite painted carving of his father's wife, the elegantly beautiful Nefertiti. And of course we see the three big triangles of the Pyramids at Gizeh.

The set of three pyramid tombs at Gizeh, with the Sphinx statue in front of them, dates from the period of 2500 BC. Tutankhamen ("King Tut") and Nefertiti lived a thousand years later. It is not archaeologists but rather the spectacle-loving public who fixate on these out of the more than three thousand years of Ancient Egyptian history. The strange, massive pyramids have always been known, and have been studied off and on by trained archaeologists for two centuries. There isn't much mystery to them; they were built to contain pharaohs' tombs to mark them forever. Burial monuments over tombs were built from the first royal dynasties in Egypt (3000 BC), gradually becoming larger and more stylized, culminating in the pyramid erected for Pharaoh Khufu (also spelled Cheops) who died in 2516 BC, with the apex of its triangle at 481 feet. Then the pharaohs turned to cutting tombs into the cliffs bordering the Nile Valley. Hundreds of these, each with piles of valuables around the mummified body in its gilded case, tempted rob-

Clockwise from top left:
—The Great Temple at Abu Simbel, carved from a mountainside near the border of Egypt with Sudan. Constructed for Ramesses II, who reigned during the 13th century BC, the temple was cut from the rock in the 1960s and shifted to higher ground to preserve it from submersion following construction of the Aswan Dam. The colossi of Ramesses II and other family members stand over 67 feet high.
—The Great Pyramids of Giza, near Cairo's outskirts.
—The Sphinx at Giza is over 4,500 years old, dating back to the Old Kingdom and time of Khafre, builder of the second largest pyramid on the Giza plateau.
—Hieroglyphs and sculptures adorn the walls of an ancient tomb found in Sakkara, "The City of the Dead," near Cairo, Egypt.

bers quite soon after each tomb was sealed. Nineteenth- and early twentieth-century archaeological expeditions to learn more about Ancient Egypt, and to unearth treasures for European and American museums to display, discovered smashed tomb doors and not much else until in 1922 when, after five years of dogged searching in this Valley of the Kings, a British archaeologist excavated a well-hidden, undisturbed burial chamber. "Everywhere the glint of gold," he told his sponsor, in spite of the body in the tomb being only a completely undistinguished royal youth, Tutankhamen, who came to the throne at the age of nine and died at eighteen, very likely of natural causes. The world being more or less at peace and prosperous in 1922, newspapers made a big deal out of the discovery, and merchandisers quickly produced King Tut souvenirs and "Egyptian style" ornaments. The tomb was kept open for tourists, hundreds of thousands of them, and every twenty years or so, museums attract a new generation by mounting a "Treasures of Tutankhamen" exhibit—the glint of gold everywhere once again.

Did the Curse of the Pharaohs kill the archaeologist? No, although his sponsor did die from an infected mosquito bite. Nor did the Curse of the Pharaohs, painted over tomb entrances, faze the thousands of robbers hacking into those tombs century after century. Do archaeologists still excavate Ancient Egyptian sites? Yes, but most often these sites are towns and villages, excavated to discover how Egyptians lived. This includes ongoing excavations at the settlements of the men who cut the rock chambers for the tombs, chiseled the monuments, and crafted precious furnishings for the royal dead. Contemporary Egyptologists have numerous papyrus documents preserved in the desert climate to give us historical detail, for example, that tomb workmen weren't always paid on time and sometimes went on strike—or resorted to robbing the tombs. Egyptology, now controlled by the government of Egypt, remains an active, if small, part of archaeology today.

STONEHENGE, THE MYSTERIOUS CIRCLE

Standing on a rolling plain in southern England is a circle of towering rough stones, the largest 25 feet high. Large stone slabs lie across the tops of several of the uprights, and another upright stone was set 33 feet to the northeast. At summer solstice, June 21 or 22, the rising sun behind this stone casts a shadow across the circle to a boulder in the center. Erected and modified between 2900 and 1600 BC, "Stonehenge" has excited visitors for as long as the Egyptian pyramids have. Unlike the pyramids, which we know were tombs for powerful rulers of a rich nation, Stonehenge has no apparent function. Western Europe-

The original purpose of Stonehenge is still unclear. It is believed to be both an astronomical observatory and a ritual structure.

ans put up many standing stones to mark the solstice by the rising sun's shadow on that day, but only at Stonehenge was the solstice marker set by such a circle of impressive stones—in fact, the circle had been in place for centuries before the solstice stone was added to the site. Puzzling, too, is why some of the great stones are sandstone from about twenty miles away, and many others are a bluish rock brought from mountains 150 miles distant. Since all the standing stones and "lintel" slabs weigh tons, how they were transported—presumably by oxen or groups of humans by dragging them along log rollers—and how they were set up—probably with wood scaffolding inserted under them, foot by foot—amazes tourists. The number of visitors to Stonehenge each year is exceeded in Britain only by the number who visit the Tower of London.

With no evidence that it was ever roofed or had real walls, Stonehenge has always been interpreted as a symbolic structure, maybe a larger-than-life temple. What significance the blue stones from distant mountains may have had, no one can guess. A long road-like embankment leads out from (or to) Stonehenge, there are other stone circles and there had been at least one wooden timber circle in the area, and there are a number of "barrows," the English term for rough stone slab tombs mounded over with earth. Archaeologists have mapped and carried out test excavations at Stonehenge and its neighbors since the beginning of the Royal Society science researches, in the late seventeenth century. Back then, it was supposed that "Druids" had constructed Stonehenge for their worship services—a belief that persists today among the public. Druids, however, were priests during the Roman era in Britain, and the Romans recorded that they conducted worship in holy groves of trees, not stone circles. It won't do to argue that the standing stones represented trees, because great effort was made to lay the lintel slabs across their tops, hardly the way to suggest groves of trees. After more than three centuries of scientific archaeology, we know in detail in what order the features of Stonehenge were constructed, but we still can't explain this most elaborate of the European prehistoric stone circles.

The Brits aren't giving up. A team of English archaeologists decided to give it a twenty-first century try, using today's high-tech methods to more precisely study the relations between Stonehenge and its Neolithic and Bronze Age neighbors on the Salisbury Plain. Tourists are now routed around the circle, after too many years of walking in it wore away soil and more stones threatened to topple. At summer solstice, hordes of police keep out people in robes who claim they are Druid priests, and flower-children types wanting to dance and drum. Away from Salisbury Plain, photos of Stonehenge appear in ads and cartoons and on computer desktops (one comes bundled with Microsoft Windows XP), there are half-size replicas in several places in America, there are "carhenges" of upended cars half-buried in circles . . . it's a symbol of the weird and mysterious. American visitors may be slightly disappointed to see that up close, the circle isn't quite so huge as it looks on those computer desktops; it is impressive, but many of our American prehistoric monuments such as the Hopewell embankments (two thousand years old) and Poverty Point in Louisiana (as old as Stonehenge) were built to greater scale.

As a postscript, Charles Darwin studied earthworms, among other organisms, and calculated that earthworm tunneling was a primary factor in causing the Stonehenge monoliths to settle deeper in the ground. In 1881, near the end of his life, Darwin published a weighty monograph on earthworms, the result of forty years' firsthand research—more than twenty years after his groundbreaking exposition of evolution through natural selection, *The Origin of Species.*

CAVE PAINTINGS

Cartoonists like Stonehenge, and they love "cavemen" painting on the walls of caves. Most people assume that before agriculture was invented, around ten thousand years ago, humans normally lived in caves. If that were so, most of the world would not have been inhabited, since caves are not available everywhere. In fact, well back in the Pleistocene (Ice Age), people constructed shelters of poles and brush, bark, or hides. Perishable though they were, archaeologists have revealed traces of such shelters forming little camps on flat open sites, even near hills where caves occur. Caves are damp and dark, and if people resorted to them, they stayed near the openings. The exception is what makes the study of cave art so thrilling: presumably for religious purposes, perhaps as long as forty thousand years ago, some humans walked, crawled, and shimmied hundreds of yards deep into pitch-dark caverns, lit torches or wicks floating in animal oil in bowl-shaped stones, and drew and painted pictures on the rock walls. Most were depictions of large animals, especially big game. In flickering lamplight, the animals seem to move. Were the painters trying to conjure to life the game they wanted to hunt?

The really astounding thing about Paleolithic (Ice Age culture) cave art is how expert most of it is. Those artists had fully human artistic talent. Seeing their art, which includes sculptures, bas-reliefs (often incorporating painting on naturally rounded protuberances resembling the animal painted), and engravings on small stones and bone and antler tools makes us appreciate that people like us, with our capacity for thought and feelings, have been around for thousands of generations. Archaeological excavations of the debris from daily life at the entrances to caves, and from valley sites, show a variety of chipped stone and bone implements for hunting, fishing, the processing of plants, preparation of hides for clothing and tents, and very likely the weaving of baskets, nets, and bags. Beads indicate the pleasure in ornaments that is so familiar to us. Experiments by archaeologists demonstrate that the stone and bone tools could be quite efficient, the main difference between them and metal tools being the greater durability of metal. The later Paleolithic people who made the art lived in communities, traded over distances of hundreds of miles, and at times attended regional assemblages, probably for games and finding lovers as well as for working out alliances and exchanges of goods and foods. All these similarities to historic nonagricultural nations, attested by the tools, food residues, and shelter traces, encourage us to interpret the cave art as part of rituals calling up from an underworld the creatures that populated their communities' world.

Paleolithic cave art was first recognized in the 1860s. Many of the caves were hidden by rock falls, and hardly any are easy to get into, so for a century few were visited. Development of tourism as an industry after the mid-twentieth century extended to popularizing cave paintings and putting in walkways and lights to draw visitors. Before long, mold and fungi grew, nourished by tourists' moist breath and the lights. France tried to protect Lascaux, one of the greatest of the ancient art galleries, by building a replica nearby and closing off the real cave. Meanwhile, archaeologists checked out newly found caves and balanced these with searches for Paleolithic paintings and engravings on valley-wall rock and on boulders. Panels of paintings were recognized in Portugal along a valley about to be flooded by a hydroelectric dam, provoking outcries to alter the dam engineering to save the ancient art. If saved, could tourists view them? Would they be safe from vandals? Cave paintings, and open-air rock paintings, preserved from thousands of years before history are thrilling links to our remote ancestors. At the same time, they are a legacy that is difficult to protect. Most of us, archaeologists included, will see these paintings via photographs in books; a few will actively research the sites.

MAYA

Thanks to Cancún and its sister high-rise hotel resorts on Mexico's east coast, Maya ruins became familiar to hordes of vacationing Americans. A couple in our town came back from a holiday eager to talk about the "mysterious" ruins at Tulúm, near Cancún. A local man who offered to be their guide informed them that the ruins had been built by extraterrestrials, come to Earth to teach humankind their civilization. Those Maya had vanished, exterminated by savage jungle tribes. *Huh?* We tried to disillusion our friends: Maya are still very much alive, their guide was probably Maya, and their civilization is known through archaeology to have developed over several thousand years, quite surely free of extraterrestrial intervention. Sad to say, the couple shook their heads: the native man surely knew more than any U.S. Ph.D.s. Well, he certainly knew how to get big tips out of tourists! Very likely he got his spiel from a popular book called *Chariots of the Gods*, written by a Swiss con man while in prison; this fellow claimed his spirit could swiftly fly anywhere to investigate ruins (helpful, considering his body was in jail).

A few years after the *Chariots* book, Alice Kehoe got a telephone call from a *National Enquirer* writer (the tabloid sold at supermarket checkouts), asking her opinion on the con man's claim that one of her sites, in Saskatchewan, Canada, was an extraterrestrial launching pad. She explained that this was doubtful, that her fieldwork indicated it was a summer solstice marker built by Indians to keep their calendar tallies accurate. The Swiss writer had never seen the site, Alice noted. "No, no, he says his spirit visited it, spent fifteen minutes on it and that's how he knows," said the tabloid journalist. Enough about psychic archaeology, for now. We will revisit the topic in chapter 6 on archaeological controversies.

The rest of us remember that scientific knowledge is limited to phenomena in the physical world. To find out about Maya, archaeologists log in sites with GIS positioning systems, map visible structures and the terrain, set up grid-control markers, hire local Maya to hack off vegetation, and then supervise them as they slowly and cautiously uncover building stones and excavate dwelling zones. The archaeologists are

Clockwise, from top left:
—Palace of Maya King Pacal, at Palenque in Mexico. Beautiful bas-reliefs and sculptures adorn the buildings and interior courts of the palace and nearby temples.
—A massive carving of the head of the Maya deity Pahuatun, Copán, Honduras.
—Archaeologist David Harris studies one of the many thousand-year-old temples at Palenque, with the goal of mapping the agricultural economy that supported the ancient city.
—The Temple of Kukulcan (El Castillo) at Chichén Itzá. Its structure marks the equinoxes and solstices of our solar year with stunning accuracy.
—A contemporary Maya family. Contrary to the opinion of proponents of psychic archaeology, the Maya people are still very much alive, speaking their Mayan language as well as Spanish and living in villages much like those of their ancestors.
—A Maya *chacmool* sculpture, Temple of the Warriors, Chichén Itzá. The bowl held by the reclining figure may have been meant to hold the hearts of sacrificial victims.

familiar with local villages where ancient, traditional types of homes, farms, cooking, and crafts have to a considerable degree persisted in spite of Spanish invasions and Mexican rule. What Spanish conquests destroyed was the indigenous writing system, a combination of hieroglyphs and phonetic signs. In the 1960s, the "code" was cracked when scholars tried reading some of the glyphs as phonetic transcriptions of Maya language. Many carved and painted inscriptions have now been read, not without difficulty due to dialect differences between Maya languages today and surely between these and the thousand-year-old, or older, texts. Inscriptions record kings and queens of the dynasties ruling Maya cities, their wars, and their alliances, while scenes carved on pillars or painted on vases illustrate a religion known through Spanish descriptions and the few Maya books not destroyed by Spanish invaders.

Maya archaeology attracts many professionals, as it does tourists, by the magnificence of its major cities adorned with sophisticated architecture and sculptures. We are full of questions, for as every researcher realizes, the more you know, the more you know you don't yet know. If you visit eastern Mexico, the Maya realm, you will be well rewarded by trips to Chichén Itzá, the intriguing city with two distinct architectural styles side by side; Palenque with its masterpieces from a nameless but extraordinarily gifted artist; or farther south in Central America, Copán or Tikal. Tulúm will do if you don't want to venture far from Cancún, although it was more a port than a rulers' capital—just avoid any local "guide" eager to tattle about extraterrestrials.

MESA VERDE

Cliff dwellings! Hidden palaces, deep within inaccessible canyons—a kid's dream, a super-tree-house. The cliff houses of Mesa Verde were designated America's first national park for archaeological ruins (1906) and are still the most popular archaeological site for tourists.

Mesa Verde's cliff houses are, in reality, a chilling lesson in human desperation, driven by war. Located in southwestern Colorado, on the Colorado Plateau at the northern border of the Southwest, these ancestral Pueblo buildings date from the late thirteenth century, when the global climate shift from the Medieval Warm Period to the Little Ice Age changed rainfall patterns in the Southwest. Along with deforestation as trees were cut over several centuries to construct thousands of Pueblo houses throughout the region, the rainfall shift facilitated erosion that reduced farmland on the plateau. Warfare that for a couple of centuries had likely been focused on getting trade advantages turned into really nasty battles for survival resources. Up until about AD 1250, most people on the Mesa Verde lived in villages on top of the mesa; then these villages were abandoned and communities retreated into wide clefts in the sheer rock walls of the canyon. Their buildings filled nearly all the available spaces in the large clefts, leaving only narrow courtyards for outdoor activities. Where did children play? Life was hard: all water was carried up steep ladders from the narrow canyon floor or from springs, with the bearer always on alert for enemy attacks. Sometimes even these naturally defensible hideouts weren't enough, as evidenced by decapitated skulls thrown into kivas.

The cliff dwellings, well preserved by their sheltered situation, were discovered in 1888 by a couple of cowboys looking for stray cattle. Fine pottery, cloth, and naturally mummified bodies attracted both scientists and looters selling to collectors, prompting a national movement for preservation that persuaded Congress to pass the first Antiquities Act in 1906, along with establishing the Mesa Verde area as a park. Visitors to the park today are introduced to the longer history of Anasazi (ancestral Pueblo) habitation on the Mesa and are guided down ladders for tours of the hidden communities.

If you visit Mesa Verde, you may want to spend another day at Chaco Canyon, to the south across the state border in New Mexico. The largest town in the prehistoric Southwest, Chaco has several multistory apartment-block pueblos and a number of smaller villages strung along the sides of a wide canyon. Three-story-high blank outer walls of the inward-facing apartment blocks defended the residents and their storehouses, without making daily life difficult as it must have been in the Mesa Verde cliff houses. Chaco flourished during the eleventh and early twelfth centuries, diminishing considerably during the century leading to the Mesa Verde cliff dwellings. It drew upon a huge outreach for building timber, turquoise to export to Mexico in exchange for scarlet macaw parrots, and food beyond what its own little desert river valley could grow. That precarious base failed after AD 1150, with a couple other Pueblo towns attempting to take over regional trade, until stable trade routes were again established, centering hundreds of miles to the south at Paquimé in the state of Chihuahua, Mexico.

—The Anasazi ("ancient ones") inhabited Mesa Verde for over 700 years, from about AD 600 to AD 1300. They built the Mesa Verde Cliff Palace, a multiple-story apartment complex with more than 200 rooms. Photo: Alice Kehoe.

—Side view of Mesa Verde Long House shows how the structures were built into the overhanging rock, making them defensible against enemies.

—Thomas Pleger at the Cliff Palace. Photo: James Gallagher.

CAHOKIA

Cahokia is the only true city built in America north of Mexico before the establishment of the United States. It lies where St. Louis, Missouri, now lies; like St. Louis, Cahokia was the hub of long-distance transportation routes between the Appalachians and the Rockies, and even beyond. It is now a UNESCO World Heritage Site, administered by the State of Illinois.

Never heard of Cahokia? Here is a real archaeological mystery: How could the ruins of a city marked by hundreds of earth mounds, the greatest towering 100 feet high, 1000 feet long and 700 feet wide, be unknown to Americans, particularly when a major interstate highway passes along its northern edge, in sight of the great mound?

The answer was figured out by Roger Kennedy, director of the Smithsonian's National Museum of American History and then director of the National Park Service. Around 1845, the United States was racked by political turmoil over slavery, industrialization, immigration, and the controversial railroads that were revolutionizing transportation. As happened before and again later, there were politicians who thought a good war would settle everything. This time, it would be conquest of Spanish California, diverting malcontents to a new frontier. A newspaperman came up with a great slogan, "Manifest Destiny." America was destined to rule from sea to shining sea. According to the British invaders who had won out over competing European powers and created the thirteen colonies that became the United States, America was a virgin wilderness with only savages incapable of civilization—Europeans had a Christian duty to take over and civilize the wilderness.

Only a few Europeans disputed that self-serving view, pointing out that America was once full of agricultural towns, many ruled by lords accorded as much pomp as any European king or queen. Thomas Jefferson personally researched the question, excavating a mound on his estate (the United States' first scientific archaeology), and commissioning explorers and educated gentlemen to record ancient ruins. But Jefferson died, and a generation later, Manifest Destiny and the Mexican War revived the conquerors' myth of a virgin wilderness. Although

—*Top:* Aerial view, looking north, of central portion of prehistoric city of Cahokia, in Illinois. Monks Mound (center of photo), 100 feet high, is one of the thousand-year-old prehistoric mounds, across the river from modern St. Louis, Missouri. It stands at the head of the Great Plaza, bordered by both round and pyramid-platform mounds. Other plazas bordered by platform mounds lay directly east, west, and north. Note the interstate freeway beyond Monks Mound in the photo. A number of Cahokia mounds were destroyed before the state of Illinois brought it into protection. Photo: Timothy R. Pauketat.

—*Bottom:* Archaeologists from Washington University (St. Louis) prepare an excavation profile of the various construction stages in Mound 34 at Cahokia for mapping and photography. Photo: Courtesy of Cahokia Mounds State Historic Site.

the first director of the Smithsonian in the 1840s struggled to carry on Jefferson's concern with our predecessors, the public and writers of history textbooks accepted the myth of a wholly primitive ancient America. First Nations' spectacular achievements in earthen architecture were not only ignored, they were bulldozed away by the thousands.

About one hundred of Cahokia's mounds survive, mostly due to nineteenth-century settlers choosing the Missouri side of the Mississippi rather than the Illinois side where the ancient city's center lies. The greatest mound, with its top larger than a football field, is called Monks Mound because in the early nineteenth century a group of Trappist monks lived on it, surrounded by simple farms. After World War II, suburban growth tapped into the farmlands: Illinois widened a road crossing Cahokia's Great Plaza, at the foot of Monks Mound, into a four-lane highway, and a subdivision of ranch homes with little backyard swimming pools was built along the east side of the plaza. One of the massive mounds bordering the plaza was destroyed to make a parking lot. Fortunately, a determined group of citizens, including some dedicated avocational archaeologists, fought the destruction and made the case to UNESCO to recognize this unique American contribution to world heritage. The State of Illinois then agreed to protect the site and more, pulling down the subdivision and creating in its place a fine museum.

Cahokia is truly an awesome place. Its urban plan of plazas ringed by high platform mounds, surrounded for miles by low mounds upon which residences had been built, and then farmsteads across the broad river bottomlands, resembles the great cities of ancient Mexico. Cahokia, like Chaco, flourished in the eleventh and early twelfth centuries AD, and as at Chaco, most of its population had dispersed by 1250. Whether the two centers were linked to each other, and how Cahokia may have been linked to Mexico, is not clear. What is patently obvious, when you visit it, is that just across the Mississippi from St. Louis, a thousand years ago, stood the capital city of an ambitious American Indian state.

Talking Points

- Can you think of other fields with a popular image that misleads people? How about movie actors? Even the great stars have to get up early, work long hours, and while away scads of time until they're needed, then repeat scenes over and over. There are very few occupations that are romantic in everyday life. On the other hand, what a person learns in depth will probably become exciting—ask an accountant or dentist who is good at his or her job.
- Why are some people so ready to believe such nonsense as the *Chariots of the Gods* account of spaceships, or mummies' curses? Are they gullible and stupid, or merely wanting a thrilling story?
- Should archaeologists pander to the public fascination with a few spectacular sites? Can we lead people on to realize the fascination of their

own local historic and prehistoric archaeology? What might help people appreciate their local heritage and see themselves as stewards responsible for conserving these cultural resources for generations to come?

- "The glory that was Greece," "the mysteries of Egypt," and "the grandeur of Rome" are phrases embedded in our culture. American First Nations, in contrast, traditionally have been labeled "savages" living in "wilderness." Is all this racism? Or is part of the problem the difficulty of appreciating ways of life different from what we grew up with? Cahokia's grandeur is less obvious, to Western eyes, than ancient Roman imperial buildings of stone, because we have not been taught to recognize the engineering feats and grand vision expressed in earth architecture.

Chapter Four

Real Archaeologists

Alice, from Girl in a Guys' World to Mom, the Professor

Working as an archaeologist is more a way of life than a matter of scheduled hours. Fieldwork usually takes the archaeologist too far from home to drive back each day. Nowadays, crews are likely to be housed in rural motels or a rented farmhouse rather than in the tent camps used years ago. Meals will more likely be of the burgers-and-spaghetti type rather than gourmet fare. After a full day in the sun troweling, measuring, sifting, and shoveling backdirt, people are ready to lie back in the summer evening, listening to someone's guitar. Come cold weather, students on crews are back in class, maybe earning credits working in the laboratory; CRM employees are in their labs sorting, analyzing, writing up reports; and professors are filtering masses of data to find significant facts. Archaeologists will be searching the ground when just walking (in Paris, gravel walkways in parks are full of good small flint nodules such as those that Paleolithic people flaked for tools). Puzzling data keep on floating up in our minds. Old buildings being torn down fascinate us, revealing structural processes and details we may not have actually seen before. The pay will never make one wealthy, but the life is rich.

Alice Kehoe first saw pictures of archaeologists in her family's *National Geographic* magazines. That was in the 1950s. Her parents brought her up to meet boys of good character, marry, and devote herself to homemaking, like her mother and grandmothers. Here's her story.

***

When I was in ninth grade, my science teacher assigned each of us to research a career in science and to make a portfolio on it. Whether the student *wanted* a career in science didn't matter. I chose archaeology and got out the back issues of my family's *National Geographics*. The teacher told me that the American Museum of Natural History in New York was running a Saturday-morning series of lectures for young people on careers in the sciences, and archaeology would be one of the presentations. We lived in a suburb of New York City, so she recommended that I attend and take notes for my assignment. This became a big deal in my home, because neither of my parents wanted to spend a Saturday going to that lecture in the city, and I, at fourteen, had never traveled into the city alone. After much discussion, they decided I could go, on my own. The lecture was given by Junius Bird, a curator of archaeology at the American Museum, and included home movies of Mrs. Bird and their little boys at the Huaca Prieta site in Peru. An eye-opener for me: a woman could be a wife and mother *and* do archaeology! And Mr. Bird was quite an attractive man.

Three not very happy years of high school followed. In the 1950s, girls were expected to be pretty and sweet, not bright. My parents planned for me to take a secretarial course, "so you can support yourself and your children if something happens to your husband." I begged and cried to be permitted to go to college; I worked summers as a temp secretary and knew those jobs would bore and frustrate me. We came to a compromise: I could go to college if I continued to live at home, and if I earned the tuition. That last wasn't so difficult because at that time, New York State gave scholarships that could be used at any accredited school in the state. I wanted to major in anthropology, not a common major then, but offered at Barnard College in New York City. For three years I commuted to Barnard, until I turned 21 and could legally leave my parents' home. My last year, I rented a room in a classmate's family's apartment near the campus.

Meanwhile, I did have a very unusual opportunity to work in the anthropology department of the American Museum, Junius Bird's department. At sixteen, when my parents expected me to get a summer job, I had the idea to write to the American Museum's anthropology department, asking whether they had summer employment for a young lady who could type (at my parents' insistence, I had taken a year-long typing course in high school). I remember my dad saying the letter was a waste of a good three-cent stamp, and my mother saying we could afford to waste three cents. Wonderful luck! The department had been granted extra funds to hire a typist to type up collection catalogs. I went in for an interview and was hired.

The catalogs were large folios of hand-written entries, the accession number, a brief description, where the object was from, and the collector's name. Some of them dated back to 1912, and all of them were the *only* record for the collections. The catalogs were kept in a vault in the department and were taken out when a researcher needed information, or when new accessions were made. It took me six weeks to type copies, including carbon copies (if I made a mistake, I had to use a razor blade to gingerly lift the carbon ink off the error and retype correctly). Once copies were typed, the original catalogs could be returned to the vault for permanent storage, and the copies put in the department office and with collections.

After my six weeks of typing, two weeks remained of August. Dr. Shapiro, chairman of the anthropology department, kindly suggested that I assist whichever curators needed aid. The following summer, I worked again in the department as an aide, and then I volunteered a day per week while attending Barnard. The summers, particularly, were fantasy fulfilled; the department at that time was highly collegial, except for the men excluding Margaret Mead, and everyone was friendly to the nice young girl.

My experience in the American Museum really set my career in archaeology, not only in providing practical experience in museum and laboratory tasks, but also in orienting me to an intellectual approach in which the challenge is to interpret empirical data, and collegial discussions are means to that end. The curators I observed—James Ford, Junius Bird, Gordon Ekholm, Harry Shapiro—and the advanced graduate student I later assisted, Walter Fairservis, believed theory should be derived from analyses of empirical data. They did not discuss abstract theories. James Ford, whom some of his contemporaries judged the most brilliant of their generation of archaeological thinkers, was at that time rebutting claims by Albert Spaulding, a professor at the University of Michigan, that statistical formulae should rule archaeological interpretation. Ford understood statistics, and he understood, with his hands that had collected and sorted thousands of sherds, that statistics are tools for the thinker; they are not god-given revelations. Spaulding converted a covey of graduate students at Michigan to his faith in numerology, and one of them, Lewis Binford, engineered what he trumpeted as the New Archaeology, supposedly a revolution in the discipline. New Archaeology claimed to be pure science, and its adherents scorned older archaeologists as "mere" culture historians. It helped the New Archaeologists that radiocarbon dating had just become available, freeing them from the hard job of figuring out age from stratigraphy and seriation (Ford's principal method). They also had the incentive of getting funds from the new National Science Foundation, if they could make their projects look really scientific. For me, New Archaeology's advocacy of advancing theoretical models to which data could then be fitted was putting the cart before the horse.

After two summers in the Museum, I wanted field experience. Angel Mounds, a Mississippian town site in southern Indiana near

Evansville, offered a well-regarded field school in archaeology that did not charge a tuition fee. The director, Glenn Black, had been a jazz musician in the 1930s when he got a job with one of the Depression relief projects in archaeology. In the 1950s, he used field-school students for his crew studying Angel Mounds. It happened that the year I enrolled, the Angel Mounds site was put on hold while the students rescued burials from a bluff-top cemetery eroding into the Ohio River upstream from Angel. There were only six of us, another young woman and four guys (including James Sackett and Robert Funk, both later prominent archaeologists). Mr. Black taught us patiently and meticulously. Decades later, a young Indiana archaeologist wanting to analyze that Yankeetown burial site found the notebooks we had prepared to be full and reliable resources. Looking back, I realize that one of the lessons I learned from Glenn Black was that good archaeologists were not necessarily Ph.D.s. His straightforward scientific method, emphasizing collection of detail, produced fruitful data for analyses and interpretation.

The next summer, I joined a project excavating a site outside Durango, Mexico. There was a small stone temple pyramid on top of a steep ridge along the Río Tunal. Durango was mostly ranch country, little explored archaeologically. J. Charles Kelley, the professor from Southern Illinois University heading the project, specialized in seeking evidence of contacts between the United States Southwest and the civilizations of Mexico. The Río Tunal site was believed, at that time, to be the northwestern-most temple pyramid in Mesoamerica. Most archaeologists working in the Southwest seemed to think Kelley somehow unpatriotic to postulate cultural and trade links south of the border, and more mainstream faculty at Southern Illinois University later made his position there difficult.

The year I was on his crew, Kelley seemed to spend day after day in town with local officials, leaving his field director, Bill, in charge of the site. Bill had a voluptuous young blond Texan wife, Dawn, who wore skintight jeans that Mexicans then considered shocking, and he had a hunky sidekick, Ed, who raced stock cars. None of us could figure out why Ed was brought along, since he didn't work, and we wondered whether one too many car crashes had affected his head—or maybe he was just dumb to begin with. A year later, Bill left archaeology to go uranium prospecting. As you may be guessing, morale at this dig was not high. Two of the young men on the crew, Mel, a medical student, and Elmo, a geology student, and I formed a threesome to spend our leisure time away from the crew, making friends with some Mexican young people, a Texan ranch owner's daughter named June who brought us out weekends to the ranch to ride, and a couple of exploration geologists with a lovely Mexican house in town. Mel, Elmo, and I bought lunch makings at the town grocery, El Numero Once, instead of eating the box meals from the hotel we were housed in, and ate most of our dinners at modest local restaurants.

After the dig was over, we went to Mexico City with June to see Teotihuacán, the great city of the first millennium AD with its immense Sun and Moon pyramids and elaborately sculpted Quezalcoatl Temple.

To make that summer even more memorable, a Hollywood Western was being filmed directly below our site's ridge, a totally forgettable film—I think it was called *White Feather*. Robert Wagner was the cowboy hero, in clothes so tight he couldn't swing his leg over a horse and had to be lifted on. Jeffrey Hunter was his Indian friend; instead of hiring an actual Indian, or at least a Chicano, the producers made the blue-eyed, Irish-descent Hunter wear brown contact lenses, shave his body, and be colored brown all over (his costume was a breechcloth). Hunter was a pleasant, intelligent man interested in the archaeological project, and he frequently joined Mel, Elmo, and me for lunch. We hinted that a movie star should contribute a few pesos to our lunch pot, but he never took the hint, just mooched off us poor students. When the Western's Indians-attacking-the-wagon-train scene was filmed, smoke from the burning wagons enveloped our site. Watching that film being shot, scenes repeated over and over, actors sitting for hours waiting for their call, convinced me that Hollywood film-making is a pretty dull enterprise.

By the summer of my third year in college, I had enough field experience to be paid $18 per week as a field assistant on a rock-shelter excavation in southern Illinois. It was then that I first encountered discrimination against women in archaeology. Men, even without prior field experience, were being hired for the Missouri River Basin Survey projects at $40 per week; women were not hired. We heard that a couple of women students had been hired for one project in an earlier year, and the notorious womanizer professor directing that project went into the tent of one of them, refusing to take her "no." She was a graduate student from New York, a woman who could not be cowed; she ran out of the tent to the road, flagged a passing car, and asked to be taken to the village police station. There she wanted to file charges of assault against the professor. The police chief told her that no one in the little town would discourage the professor, whose purchases of food and supplies for his crew were a windfall for local merchants. She left the dig, and after that, River Basin Surveys claimed women were troublemakers and shouldn't be hired. Never mind the second young woman on the dig, who had a boyfriend there to protect her, and was, the professor said at the end of the summer, the best on the crew!

When I was about to graduate from Barnard, I applied to three graduate programs in anthropology, at Harvard, University of Pennsylvania, and University of Chicago. Penn did not accept me, Harvard did, and I decided I'd prefer Cambridge, Massachusetts, to Chicago. I also applied for a summer job as assistant at the Museum of the Plains Indian on the Blackfeet Reservation in Montana, adjacent to Glacier National Park. The job circular was odd, asking for only women who were recent anthropology majors, requesting their height, weight, age, and a photo. My Barnard anthropology professor wrote me a recommendation, mentioning that among my skills was cooking. I was selected.

The Museum of the Plains Indian had two staff people, the Blackfoot maintenance man and Tom Kehoe, director and also curator, 29 years old, single, hoping to find a helpmate for life as an archaeologist. Smart guy! He used the federal employment form to choose a likely young woman from the applicants for the summer job. Unlike the River Basin Survey professor, Tom was mindful of appropriate conduct, but we were together most of the time, there being little to do in Browning, the reservation town. Evenings, Tom drove me to see the nearer sections of Glacier Park, and we picnicked. The museum had been built as a WPA project in the Depression, with the bulk of its collection of Plains Indian costumes and manufactures donated by heirs of the Great Northern Railroad magnate James J. Hill. The railroad crossed the Blackfeet Reservation, and Hill built grand hotels in Glacier Park to attract passengers, hiring Blackfoot families to camp in tipis between the railroad station and adjacent hotel in East Glacier, dance, and pose for photos with tourists. Two years before I came out, Museum Director Claude Schaeffer expanded the staff to include an archaeologist to survey the reservation; Schaeffer hired Tom Kehoe, who was completing a master's degree in anthropology at the University of Washington. The next year, Schaeffer became ill and resigned, leaving young Tom as director, curator, and archaeologist. That crunch enabled him to get funds for an assistant for the summer tourist season.

By the end of the summer, Tom and I decided to marry. Coincidentally, he was planning to attend Harvard for his Ph.D. after completing his Master's thesis for the University of Washington. Harvard agreed to let me postpone my entrance a year, to go with Tom, and we settled in the comfortable cottage attached to the Museum. Tom's thesis was about tipi rings, the circles of stones lying by hundreds of thousands over the Plains, rolled off Indian tipis when they were pulled up. An archaeologist at the University of Wyoming had opined that this explanation for the circles was only folklore, that it was scientific to consider them "manifestations of unknown relationships." Dr. Schaeffer, considering the folk explanation probably true, helped Tom design a field survey, test excavations, interview Indian elders, and do library research to discover the best interpretation. All Tom's work indicated the Wyoming professor was not justified in rejecting the folk identification. Once the Museum's summer tourist season ended, I helped Tom with some of the tipi-ring excavations, sat in on interviews, and labored beside him as he organized his data and wrote up the sections of the thesis. Then I typed it, as good wives did in those days. The thesis was accepted by the University of Washington, and on the recommendation of our Harvard professor, J. O. Brew, published by the Smithsonian in its Anthropological Papers series (1960). It remains a landmark in Plains archaeology.

PROFESSIONAL LIFE

Tom was a very sound archaeologist with a talent for operationalizing research questions. The second summer of our marriage, he began excavation at a bison kill site near Browning, expecting to recover weapon points in stratigraphic sequence from the layers of kills, and from them chart a chronology of styles for the Northwestern Plains. It happened that the recently established Glenbow Museum in Calgary, Alberta, a couple hundred miles north of Browning, had just hired an archaeologist, and he would be excavating a comparable bison kill in Alberta. After two seasons' work, we three compared results and were gratified to see that the sequences of weapon point styles deposited in these sites over centuries were parallel. Each excavator also obtained some radiocarbon dates, providing benchmark dates for the sequences. This pair of projects, the Boarding School Drive in Montana and the Old Women's Jump in Alberta, laid the foundation for Late Prehistoric period archaeology of the Northwestern Plains. Tom subsequently extended the sequence through excavations at the Gull Lake bison kill site in southwestern Saskatchewan. For his significant archaeological projects and pioneering work as Saskatchewan's first provincial archaeologist, the Plains Anthropological Conference awarded him its Distinguished Service plaque in 2004.

I, of course, took part in these projects. For the Boarding School report, I analyzed the loads of butchered bison bones from the several corrals the prehistoric Indians had built under a bluff the herds had stampeded over. From the National Bison Range we got the skeleton of an old bison bull, and from the Crow Indian Reservation's meat herd, those of a cow and calf for me to use in identifying age, sex, and patterns of butchering. Tom had learned the value of analyzing butchered bone from a zoologist who was on a River Basin Survey project with him. Zooarchaeology is an integral subfield in archaeology now, but it was rare back then. For the Gull Lake project, we hired a young woman archaeology student to sort butchered bone and write up identifications on charts Tom prepared, freeing me to direct the fieldwork during Tom's absences to check on other projects in the province. That first season at Gull Lake, I also cooked for the crew, assisted by the bones analyst; that turned out to be more than we reasonably could handle. It did help that we had an older man on the crew as a volunteer, and he frequently remarked at dinner that the dish served was "really flavorful!" The crew boys would look surprised but stifle their rude remarks. I could see that John was taking the lead in keeping up morale and thanked him, whereupon he confided that "really flavorful!" meant "strong flavor, maybe a disagreeable flavor!"

In between summer excavations, Tom and I spent semesters in Cambridge attending Harvard. They were difficult periods for us, partly because we had so little money and the cost of living was so high, partly because the professors in the anthropology department considered Plains archaeology uninteresting and women not worth bothering with. It was obvious, too, that men from wealthy, socially well-connected families were favored. Tom's family was made up of farmers and factory workers from Janesville, a small city in southern Wisconsin, mine mostly of small business people, although my father was a lawyer. Disrespect irritated Tom, and he did not get along with most of the faculty, J. O. Brew excepted (Brew was himself disrespected for lack of family money or social status).

The "benign neglect" given to all the women students didn't bother me, since it was clearly extended to all of us women and was what I had been accustomed to everywhere except at Barnard, the women's college. We women graced the classes and did grunt work, and in time would marry and disappear; if we married a fellow anthropologist, we would be the silent partner in research and writing. A few women tried to assert their worth, but when requests came to recommend candidates for jobs, men were routinely selected. The 1964 Civil Rights Act changed women's position in law, quite slowly in practice. Harvard was formally censured by the American Anthropological Association for its bias against women, yet Harvard is still notorious for the preponderance of men on its faculty.

Being a woman student at Harvard was discouraging enough, without the burden I carried of being a mother, too. Baby Danny wasn't planned, at least so soon in our marriage, but very much wanted. Another graduate student's wife took in babies to watch with her own, giving me time to attend classes, and Miss Currier, the librarian for Anthropology, bent the rules to let me take books out overnight, hidden under Danny's blanket in the pram. My best friend and classmate from Barnard, Dena Ferran Dincauze, was another wife-and-mother at Harvard. We could get together with our babies, and a few other impecu-

Clockwise from top left:

—Alice doing the dinner dishes in field camp, Saskatchewan. When the dishes and pots were done, she would write up the day's fieldnotes. Photo: Thomas F. Kehoe.

—Alice interviewing Mr. Joe Douquette, a Cree First Nation Indian, about interpretation of the Moose Mountain boulder construction. Mr. Douquette said that early in Cree history in Saskatchewan, his nation had priests who observed the movements of the sun by means of natural features such as hills and kept calendars based on summer solstice as New Year. Photo: Thomas F. Kehoe.

—Blackfoot elders examining the excavated bison drive. Their grandparents had seen the last bison drives, in the 1870s. At the time the Kehoes were working at the Boarding School site, it was not yet common to consult local Indian people when interpreting archaeological data. Photo: Alice Kehoe.

—The Boarding School bison drive. Drawing: Jerry Livingston.

—Excavated corral, Boarding School bison drive. A corral pole lies at lower right, beside butchered bison bones. Preservation of wood like this pole is unusual. Photo: Alice Kehoe.

—Alice excavating a tipi ring, Blackfeet Reservation, Montana. Photo: Thomas F. Kehoe.

nious students would join us to talk about our courses. Dena came from Massachusetts and was determined to research New England prehistory, never mind our professors telling her that nothing was left to discover. She sought out local avocational archaeologists and found that there were many eager to work with her, wrote a couple of basic monographs on ancient New England, and with recommendation from a professor we had studied with at Barnard, made her mark editing the Society for American Archaeology's journal, *American Antiquity*. Dena became the Society's third woman president, the first to be a mother.

Come the day to talk with our major professor, Dr. Brew, about our dissertation topics, I was in for another blow. Tom, by that time Saskatchewan provincial archaeologist, proposed to excavate the Gull Lake site, known from testing to hold many layers of occupation. I proposed to excavate François' House, a fur trade post on the other side of Saskatchewan. Tom and I had been careful throughout our coursework to establish ourselves independently, and we selected our dissertation projects to be dissimilar, far apart in space and time and relevance. Professor Brew shook his head. "Alice, you'll have to do your dissertation in ethnography. Otherwise, people will say Tom did it for you." "But Dr. Brew, we're going to be working on these sites at the same time. No one can simultaneously excavate two big sites, hundreds of miles apart, and write them up for dissertations!" "I understand, and I would accept these projects, but other people won't. Surely you can find something there in Saskatchewan for an ethnographic study." Professor Brew really believed he was protecting me, giving me a chance to be a professional anthropologist instead of merely Tom's wife. Perhaps he was right.

Back in Saskatchewan, I talked to people familiar with Indians in the province. (Ethnography at that time meant studying non-Western peoples. Not until the 1970s did it become acceptable that anthropologists observe European or American communities.) Someone mentioned hearing that a Ghost Dance shirt had come from a Dakota reserve. That might lead to a dissertation, since no one had reported the Ghost Dance movement in Canada. I inquired on the four Dakota reserves in the province and discovered that Sioux Wahpeton, outside Prince Albert, did have a congregation of followers of the Ghost Dance religion. No magically bullet-proof shirt ever turned up, but to find living believers was startling. Textbooks stated that the Ghost Dance religious movement lasted only a few years in the 1890s, destroyed by the massacre of a Lakota camp at Wounded Knee, South Dakota. Here indeed was a great topic for a dissertation, and research that was feasible for a woman with kids. My dissertation was accepted, without any of the Harvard professors thinking it worth mentioning.

Now, Ph.D. secured, I could excavate the fur trade post. François LeBlanc and his partner, James Finlay, built a set of cabins on the Saskatchewan River in 1768, the first successful Euro-Canadian post in the province. Because their operation was illegal in territory monopolized by the Hudson's Bay Company (HBC), no records survive. A Canadian historian had traveled the river with copies of the Hudson Bay Company employees' journals, tramping along the banks wherever landscapes seemed to match descriptions in the journals. An HBC man spying on the competition had visited François' House, enabling the historian to locate it. Our two seasons' excavations revealed the post's log buildings and range of trade goods and local Indian manufactures, providing a baseline of securely dated artifacts that would help identify other Protohistoric sites in the province. Now we had an outline of artifact types from AD 200, the lowest occupation layer at Gull Lake, to 1773 when François and Finlay moved their operation upriver. I was particularly intrigued by the Indian women's tools and pots in François' House, testimony to the "country wives" living with the traders. When in the 1970s a few of my feminist colleagues promoted "gendering" archaeology, to identify women's activities and roles from the archaeological record (and by default, men's activities), I had data to contribute.

Saskatchewan in the 1960s was governed by the CCF, an agrarian socialist political party. Their populist socialist principles had led to establishing the provincial archaeology program that brought us there. Another innovation was introducing a provincial health insurance program covering everyone, on the model of Britain's National Health Service. Conservative doctors, especially the American Medical Association, fought hard against the program, fearing it would affect their incomes. There was a doctors' strike. Then, that failing, the AMA allied with one of Canada's conservative parties to challenge the CCF in provincial elections. Pouring unprecedented monies and advertising into the campaign, the conservatives ousted the CCF. The new government had no interest in heritage programs, ordering Tom to stay in his office and give up fieldwork. I had just been given a one-course introductory anthropology teaching job at the University of Regina, expecting the next year to have a regular appointment, when the CCF-supporter historian who had hired me left the province and I was told by his successor that none of his friends, myself included, would ever teach there. Tom and I were deeply disappointed at these political repercussions. We felt we had no choice but to leave Saskatchewan.

For three years, we lived in Lincoln, Nebraska, where I taught anthropology and Tom was director of the Nebraska Historical Society Museum. Tom was miserable being stuck in administration, and when my department chairman admitted (several years after the 1964 Civil Rights Act), "I'll never give a tenure-track contract to a woman," we looked for new jobs. A friend at Milwaukee Public Museum let us know that he planned to take an academic position, advising us that if we were Milwaukee residents, Tom would get preference applying for the museum position. Marquette University in Milwaukee also had an opening for an anthropologist. Milwaukee Public Museum, one of the top natural history museums, had been Tom's boyhood dream job, and we liked the city. Marquette hired me, we moved, and soon Tom became curator of archaeology in the Milwaukee Public Museum. My new department chairman not only gave me a proper contract and fair salary but also willingly accommodated my family obligations by assigning me class times coinciding with the children's school schedules.

Once again able to organize field projects, Tom signed us on as volunteers on an excavation at the classic Upper Paleolithic site of Solutré in eastern France. With thousands of butchered reindeer and wild horse bones under a steep cliff, the site was believed to have been similar to Plains Indian bison drive sites. We knew those sites intimately, having excavated three major ones and tested or mapped many others. Could we confirm the French site based on our American experience? We did: driving herd game over carefully selected drop-offs into corrals was an Upper Paleolithic invention eventually brought to America. At the end of the summer, we joined a tour of famous French Paleolithic sites led by the legendary, brilliant and irascible professor François Bordes. Reading about archaeology can't match actually seeing sites, especially ongoing excavations.

Several subsequent summers we spent in Saskatchewan, on smaller archaeological and ethnographic projects. Our kids came with us, playing in the backdirt when they were little, helping a bit when older, mostly just being outdoors, watching dragonflies and eating saskatoon berries from the bushes, much like Indian kids they saw when we visited reserves for the National Museum of Canada's Urgent Ethnography Programme. One summer, we camped near a northern Cree family fishing and hunting, observing how their activities might leave an archaeological residue—"ethnoarchaeology," except that we weren't able to do the final stage of returning years later to their camp, to confirm what did result. Another two summers, we worked at a unique site, the Moose Mountain "Medicine Wheel." High on an upland ridge overlooking the plains, it was a configuration of small boulders in lines radiating from a

Clockwise, from top left:

—Moose Mountain site, Saskatchewan, excavated center of central cairn, showing large white rock (upper left) that originally stood on top for sighting solstice. Over the centuries, passersby added stones (upper right) to the cairn, obscuring its purpose. Charcoal bits from the cairn's base (identification tag) gave a radiocarbon date of first millennium BC. Photo: Alice Kehoe.

—Measuring the central rock cairn. Photo: Alice Kehoe.

—Sighting summer solstice at Moose Mountain. After 2,000 years, shift in earth's axis makes it appear that the sun rises on the east edge of the central cairn; originally, it rose directly over the big white rock now buried under later additions of stones. Photo: Alice Kehoe.

—Map of Moose Mountain "medicine wheel" site featuring astronomical sight lines. Drawing: Alice Kehoe.

—The central rock cairn, and one of the rock alignments. Photo: Alice Kehoe.

—Alice excavating near the central rock cairn. Plastic sheets are used to protect excavated areas. Photo: Thomas F. Kehoe.

Aldebaran
A
Solstice Sunrise
Capella
B
F
Sirius
C
E
D
Fomalhaut

central stone cairn. Tom had realized that the radiating lines matched some of those in the Big Horn Medicine Wheel on a similar high ridge in Wyoming, a site provocatively identified by an astronomer as a means of determining summer solstice (similar to the Heel Stone at Stonehenge).

Tom sent our map of the Moose Mountain structure to the astronomer, and he agreed to meet us there at summer solstice, to get the crucial angles and watch the sun come up at the site. We enjoyed assisting in research new to us, our collaborator being a good camper and a scientist who knew when to be precise and when precision isn't justified. His conclusion left us skeptical: His measurements indicated that the structure gave lines of sight to *six* stars, including our sun, on summer solstice or within a month before or after, *at two thousand years ago*! Earlier or later, not all star positions would be lined up. The next summer, Tom and I excavated portions of the structure (with permission of the Indian band that had title to the land), finding charcoal bits we could submit for radiocarbon dating. Our collaborator's conclusion was validated with radiocarbon dating of first millennium BC, two thousand or so years ago. Moose Mountain is evidence that back in Hopewell times, even out on the northern Plains, Indian people maintained astronomical records enabling them to keep a reliable calendar.

WORKING INDEPENDENTLY

Then, in the 1980s, Tom surprised and dismayed me by losing interest in archaeology, in his museum job, in me. He had spent a year in Germany as a Fulbright professor, a year in which he ate poorly and exercised little. He became plump, moody, restless; he started seeing another woman. It took several years before he felt ill and consulted a doctor who diagnosed diabetes. Constant low blood sugar from impaired insulin production had caused Tom to feel depressed. Under the doctor's regime, he managed the diabetes, but by that time his lady friend wasn't giving him up. When our youngest left home for college, Tom and I divorced.

Minus my companion in archaeology, I needed to come up with research I could carry out alone. Our support for fieldwork had been officially granted to Tom, leaving me without a record of successful grants. There wasn't much hope of my breaking into the grants game from a university with only a tiny undergraduate anthropology program—and as a woman, middle-aged to boot. About this time, Joan Gero, a graduate student in archaeology at the University of Massachusetts, had checked records for National Science Foundation grants to archaeologists and discovered that men were five times more likely than women to be awarded funds, and that what did go to women was almost always for laboratory analyses, not directing field projects. The NSF archaeology programs director confessed he hadn't noticed the gross bias and promised to try to correct it in future. Well and good, thought I, but right now, no point in trying to launch my own field project.

One of my Marquette undergraduate students, Alan Kolata, had gone on to become director of a substantial, multi-year, NSF-supported archaeological project in highland Bolivia at the great ancient city of Tiwanaku. During surveys of surrounding countryside, Kolata was intrigued by regular rows of low ridges near Lake Titicaca. Hypothesizing these were once raised beds for agriculture, he persuaded villagers to rebuild a few and gave them seed potatoes to plant on them. The harvest was phenomenal. Kolata wanted to extend the restoration of ancient field systems the following year, but villagers insisted they would work only for cash wages. That, he couldn't squeeze out of his budget. Alan and I had kept in touch, and he confided to me his disappointment. "What does the ethnographer for your project report?" I asked him. "We don't have any ethnographer." "No one in the villages, listening to what people say and observing daily life?" "No, though I've tried to get graduate students to go." Alan's venture had potential to put tons of food in the dishes of really poor communities. I had a sabbatical leave coming up. I proposed I'd spend some months living in one of the villages, recording what they ate, how they obtained food, and how they felt about the raised-fields restorations. Although I did not speak Aymara, the local Indian language, younger people in the villages could converse with me in Spanish.

What transpired was that the villagers, desperate for money, had been holding out on Alan although they intended to work on the restorations and get all the seed potatoes they could, even if he didn't give in on wages. Living, eating, and working on the raised beds with them, I convinced them that "Doctor Alán" really didn't have the money they wanted, and he would have paid them if he could. With the first year's great harvests repeated, the Bolivian government took notice and instituted an extension program teaching the method to hundreds of villages. Alan's vigorous efforts to raise funds for his pilot program brought him to the notice of the Smithsonian, and a delightful outcome was that my friends from the village were invited, expenses paid, to participate in a summer Folklife Festival on the Mall in Washington, DC.

My sabbatical year was half over when I returned from the Andes. The second half of leave could hardly be a greater contrast: Edinburgh, Scotland. History of archaeology took off as a subfield in the late 1980s, catalyzed by a scholarly conference at Southern Illinois University. As I taught introductory archaeology and grappled with questions of scientific validity—were the hotshot New Archaeologists justified in scorning the men I had assisted at the American Museum?—I suspected that a sociology-of-knowledge approach would clarify issues. Sir

John Lubbock, regularly cited as the founder of scientific prehistoric archaeology in the 1860s, was not, I discovered, the first in this field, but rather an imitator of a Scotsman, Daniel Wilson. Wilson's 1851 *Archaeology and Prehistoric Annals of Scotland* introduced the word "prehistory" into English, and I was excited to find that he soon after emigrated to Canada, visited American sites and studied collections, and canoed Lake Superior with Ojibwe to learn how these First Nations people lived in their forests. His second book, *Prehistoric Man*, contained substantial accounts of American antiquities, presented with respect for our First Nations' technologies and ways of life. Sir John Lubbock, comfortable in his English mansion, called American Indians "savages." Was it the popularity of such racist views that made Lubbock more palatable to readers, or was it simply that Lubbock was rich, influential, and living in London, while Daniel Wilson came from an impoverished family and lived far away in America?

Seeing a circular on an Institute for Advanced Studies in the Humanities at Edinburgh University, I applied for, and received, a fellowship during my sabbatical. Not only would I be able to research Daniel Wilson's earlier work, I would be able to discuss my material with innovative sociologists of science in Edinburgh's Science Studies Unit. Their approbation of my focus on the social context of Wilson's and Lubbock's books gave me confidence to extend the approach into twentieth-century American archaeology. My research revealed that Wilson had been an active part of a Scottish political reform movement in the 1840s, attempting to dislodge aristocratic privilege in favor of merit-based advancement. In spite of America's love of democracy, the same struggle took place here, as Tom and I and our friends had experienced at Harvard. History books that chronicle the triumph of a ruling political party are called "Whig histories," after the British conservative party; the book I wrote, *A Critical History of American Archaeology*, is the opposite, giving Wilson his deserved place in the history of archaeology and presenting ideas that the bigwigs of archaeology shove under the rug.

Back in 1977, my close friend and colleague David Kelley and I had convened a two-week scholarly conference in Mexico to discuss evidence of trans-Pacific contacts between Asia and Mesoamerica before Columbus. Gordon Ekholm, at the American Museum, had argued that some parallels could best be explained by such voyages. Way before us, the great early-nineteenth-century naturalist Alexander von Humboldt had described such parallels, postulating pre-Columbian contacts, and in our time, so had Joseph Needham, a Cambridge University scholar noted for his pioneering work in biochemistry and then, retired from his lab, a second career as historian of Chinese science and technology. Kelley and I had the bold idea of inviting Needham to meet with archaeologists at Mexican sites and museums to objectively evaluate, firsthand, these parallels and similarities. Needham, although 77 years old, was eager to do so. He proved to be an exceptionally humble person, in spite of his powerful intellect and many honors; he insisted we all, even the two children in our group, address him as "Joseph." Our two weeks' face-to-face confrontations with hard evidence convinced Joseph, as well as Ekholm, Kelley, our colleague Paul Tolstoy, and myself, that von Humboldt had been right. The several more conventional American archaeologists we had invited stuck to the standard dogma that no one could have crossed the Pacific before sixteenth-century Europeans. (How could they be blind to the fact that Polynesians sailed over thousands of miles of ocean to every habitable island?)

Joseph Needham's career switch from biochemistry to historian of science seemed to him unremarkable: He was thinking as a scientist in his lab, and he was thinking as a scientist as he read Chinese books on technologies and philosophies of knowledge. One afternoon, he told me how he understood life: It is like swimming along a river, carried by the current, sometimes rapidly forward, sometimes into a backwater eddy to slowly drift out, sometimes in clear water, sometimes in murky. Tributaries from time to time enter and enrich the river. Rocks loom up, and if one tries too hard to swim against the current to avoid them, one is knocked and bruised, but if one doesn't struggle too hard, the current will carry one around the obstacle. At the end, we float into the boundless sea. When my life was changing with Tom's rejection and our children grown, I reflected on Joseph Needham's metaphor.

The current of my life now carries me back to the Montana Blackfeet Reservation on extended visits, alongside writing that draws on my wide experiences. Professor Brew's insistence on my doing ethnography set me afloat for producing a textbook, *North American Indians: A Comprehensive Account*, integrating pre-contact archaeological culture histories with First Nations ethnohistories. Keeping abreast of developments in Indian Country, with my friends on the Blackfeet Reservation and my anthropologist colleagues who are American Indians, provides a perspective on archaeological practices and presuppositions.

One of my continuing research concerns is with identifying fabrics impressed on pottery. Most archaeologists call these "cord-impressed," not wanting to take the time to closely examine imprints to discover what fabrics were made, although for most of ancient America these sherds are our only record of such perishables. Observing my Blackfoot friends keeping religious items in handwoven bags much like the fabrics I see impressed on their forebears' pottery, I know that describing fabrics from the archaeological record, however tedious, is part of archaeologists' responsibility toward data. My long-standing engagement with fabrics in the record alerted me to likely misidentification of Upper Paleolithic bone artifacts, conventionally labeled "projectile points" but hardly strong enough for such use, and resembling weaving shuttles and net-making tools I'd seen in ethnographic collections. To investigate this, I went to the Czech Republic to participate in an Upper Paleolithic excavation and examine museum artifacts. Bone objects suited to fabric manufacture are common in later Upper Paleolithic collections, suggesting this was when fiber products—twined or woven cloth, netting—were invented.

The Moravian Museum (Brno, Czech Republic) also has, as a special treasure, a set of tiny Paleolithic mammoth-ivory carvings always labeled "mammiform pendants" (in crude English, boob-shaped pendants). The single complete finished specimen has a ring for suspension carved on the back. Hmm . . . how did it look suspended? I put a string through the ring and held it up. Omigosh! The way it dangled, *it wasn't "mammiform"*! Quite the contrary—it was an accurately carved representation of human male genitalia! Somehow, none of the gentlemen archaeologists had tried suspending it as it was designed, and instead looked at the pendant backward, mistaking testicles for breasts. When I put it to the Czech archaeologist hosting me, he was upset and told me I should not disturb the respected museum director. So much for truth, not to mention recognizing gender in archaeology.

Looking back, the river of my life seems to have flowed steadily, deepening and carrying an ever-increasing variety of good things. Have I had a typical career as an archaeologist? Yes and no. Yes, in that I earned my Ph.D., taught for many years in a university, carried out field projects, and published reports on them. No, in that not many archaeologists have done as much ethnography as I have—almost a dual career path. My "excuse" is that in the region of my primary fieldwork, the Northwestern Plains, "prehistory," doesn't end until the bison herds were exterminated in the 1880s. Tom and I interviewed a very old Blackfoot lady who remembered what it was like, as a child, to live in a bison-hide tipi and leaving a tipi ring when it was moved. Archaeology moves the past into the present. My life in archaeology illustrates a range of topics one can pursue, lured by a world full of curious objects somehow related to human lives.

Talking Points

- As recently as 2003, a survey of members of the Society for American Archaeology revealed that relatively few men perceived discrimination against women in the profession, while half the women respondents did see discrimination in funding; invitations to participate in conference sessions, scholarly meetings, and publications; and promotions. Interestingly, a majority of both men and women responded that the most serious problem they perceived is "juggling a family and a career" (Baxter 2005:8). This SAA survey indicates archaeology is not different from other professions, and circumstances not as radically changed from pre-Civil Rights Act times as women expected.

- Some archaeologists focus narrowly on one region, time period, or type of artifact (stone, pottery, metal). They may become known as authorities on their chosen focus. We think this is a matter of personality as well as opportunity.

Chapter Five

Real Archaeologists
Thomas, the Next Generation

My journey to becoming a professional archaeologist started at a very young age. I grew up on the shores of Lake Michigan in the small Midwestern city of Marinette, Wisconsin. Marinette has approximately 12,000 people and is located in northeast Wisconsin along the border with the Upper Peninsula of Michigan.

My mother and father were both college educated and my father was a practicing attorney. He had a particular interest in archaeology, and he had worked on an archaeological excavation in the area in the 1960s. In the early 1970s, my family moved to a home along the shoreline of Lake Michigan. My father thought that we would someday find archaeological materials along the water's edge, since this area was known to be the homeland of the Menominee Indians in early historic times. One day while raking our beach, Dad came into the house with a handful of lithic fragments. He was convinced that the stones in his hands were debris from manufacturing stone tools. Shortly thereafter, he found a small triangular flaked stone arrow point, then several more. I was extremely interested in the artifacts that Dad found so close to our home. I imagined what my neighborhood would have looked like in prehistoric times. In the 1970s, the shoreline was dotted with middle-class family homes. I was fascinated, thinking how people could have survived in this environment where winter temperatures regularly dip more than 20 degrees below zero and summer can see temperatures in the 90s. Winter must have been particularly challenging for prehistoric Indians in this region.

Together, my father and I began to collect artifacts along the shoreline. My mother joined in, and one of my childhood friends collected with us. The materials were in secondary context, moved by lake changes, so it was difficult to determine if all of the stone, bone, copper, and ceramic artifacts belonged to one culture or many. Over time, my father and I started to attend archaeological meetings, read journals, and meet professional archaeologists. Through these contacts, we began to realize that the artifacts we had recovered came from many different prehistoric cultures spanning at least 5000 years. Above all, I came to appreciate the value of reporting anything we noticed to our regional archaeologists, and engaging their guidance.

While in high school, I enrolled in an archaeology field school at the University of Wisconsin-La Crosse. UWL is a mid-sized public university located in the scenic Mississippi River Valley of southwestern Wisconsin. This area is a very rich ecological zone and was heavily occupied by American Indians throughout prehistory. The field school introduced me to professional archaeological methods of excavation and data recovery. We worked on a Hopewell burial site that was approximately 2000 years old. Hopewell refers to a series of cultures that lived near river systems in Midwestern North America from approximately 100 BC to AD 400. Hopewell peoples were hunter-gatherer-gardeners who participated in an elaborate exchange or trade system that connected people from as far away as the southeastern United States to the western Great Lakes and beyond.

The site, showing remnants of a series of mounds, was particularly intriguing because Hopewell people buried their dead in earthen tumuli with subfloor burial pits. At this site, the mounds had been plowed away over many years of farming, but burials remained intact below the plow zone. I was only on the project for a few weeks, but it convinced me that archaeology was a fascinating field. Professional archaeology requires curiosity, great patience, good critical thinking skills, and a love of the outdoors. Through the project, I met professors Jim Gallagher, Jim Theler, and regional archaeologist Robert "Ernie" Boszhardt, who would become my teachers, mentors, colleagues and good friends.

Due in part to my experience in their field school, I decided to enroll at the University of Wisconsin-La Crosse as a freshman, just out of high school in the late 1980s. I knew the university had plenty of archaeology courses and the faculty was first rate, but at the time I did not realize that they lacked a formal anthropology or archaeology major. There were probably fewer than a dozen students who were interested in archaeology as a career. I started by taking introductory courses, and by my second semester I was hooked and enrolled in a number of upper-level anthropology and archaeology classes. Once I realized there was no formal anthropology major, I decided to major in political science and minor in anthropology. The two fields were at least somewhat related, both social sciences, and I also figured that law might be good backup if archaeology did not pan out.

While at UWL, I was able to work on many different sites in the Upper Mississippi River Valley. The City of La Crosse was built on top of a large number of late-prehistoric Indian villages inhabited by an archaeological culture called Oneota, who flourished in the region from about AD 1300 to AD 1625. The communities raised corn and hunted, fished, and gathered wild foods. As modern La Crosse expanded in the late 1980s, many developments encroached on archaeological sites. As a consequence, there were plenty of opportunities to work on archaeological sites that needed to be investigated under state and federal laws requiring archaeological investigation prior to construction.

UW-La Crosse was a great place to study archaeology. Classes were small, professors were engaging, and learning archaeology first-hand in the field was readily available. These experiences taught me much about what it was like to work on real-world field projects. Often during the summer, we labored on excavations or surveys in heat and humidity, in areas covered with poison ivy and/or infested with mosquitoes, especially along the Mississippi River. While at UWL, I met my spouse, Teresa, a health education major. She would play a big role in helping me become a professional archaeologist.

At UWL, I made it a point to get the most out of my education by attending lectures on archaeology and anthropology outside of classes, getting to know most of my professors, and spending a semester overseas. The University of Wisconsin runs a small campus located in an eighteenth-century palace in Dalkeith, Scotland, a small town located just outside of Edinbrough. In the spring of 1989, I went over with my undergraduate major professor, Dr. Jim Gallagher, to study British archaeology. It was a fantastic experience—I would recommend that every undergraduate spend at least a few weeks studying overseas. Taking courses on the archaeology of the British Isles, I was able to find part-time employment on an excavation, by the University of Glasgow, of a Roman fort occupied during the first century AD. The site was just outside the campus, and the crew had exposed some masonry by the time I arrived. It was very different from what I was used to in the States: there were so many artifacts, very little was screened, and pottery sherds were rarely saved unless they were decorated. The project revealed fortress walls, living quarters, and other buildings from the Roman occupation of Britain.

After undergraduate school, I had planned to attend law school and combine archaeology and law. I thought that, given the development of historic preservation law in the United States to protect and manage both archaeological and historic sites, there would be need for lawyers with background in archaeology. I applied to several law schools, did not get into either my first or second choice, and decided that I should continue with my interests in archaeology, pursuing a master's degree in anthropology and then going on to law school. My parents and my wife encouraged me to aim for the University of Wisconsin-Madison anthropology master's program.

UW-Madison is the largest of the twenty-six University of Wisconsin campuses, with approximately 42,000 students. It is the second largest producer of Ph.D.s (total number in all fields) in the United States and has a top-ten anthropology/archaeology program. I was not quite sure just how best to apply, so I contacted my undergraduate professors at UWL. Both of my archaeology professors wrote letters of recommendation and called Dr. James Stoltman, the Midwestern archaeologist at UW-Madison. I then talked to Dr. Stoltman by telephone and arranged for an interview. My wife Teresa and I drove down to Madison; to us it seemed a huge city compared to the communities we had lived in. I had graduated with honors from UWL and knew my undergraduate professors were highly supportive of me continuing to graduate school, so I thought I would at least have a chance of getting accepted.

I remember walking up Bascom Hill, the heart of the campus, to the massive Social Science Building. Hundreds of students of all ages walked up and down the sidewalks as I headed up the hill. The campus was so enormously larger than UWL! I found the fifth floor of the Social Science building where the Anthropology Department was located, then found Dr. Stoltman's office. He greeted me and we began to talk about why I wanted to study archaeology at the University of Wisconsin, asking a number of questions about my goals and interests in anthropology. I explained my interests in Wisconsin archaeology, told him that I wanted so much to come to Madison, that I would work very hard and who knows, maybe I would change my mind and want to pursue a Ph.D. He pulled out a handwritten list of classes and told me he would see me in several weeks when classes began. I was in!

Studying archaeology at UW-Madison was exciting and challenging. For the first time, I only took classes related to my interests. I had about a dozen fellow new graduate students (those students pursuing a post-baccalaureate degree). They were from both private and public universities from around the country. I found many of them to be exceptionally bright, hard-working, and equally as excited about archaeology as I was. While at Madison, I took courses on archaeological method and theory, the origins of humanity in terms of both biology and culture, and various regional courses focusing on the prehistory of selected areas of the world, including Mesoamerica, Europe, Africa, North America, and Wisconsin. Some of the more interesting seminar courses included an experimental archaeology course where we learned how to make stone tools, and to build and fire our own clay pots; for this course I conducted my own experiments in prehistoric copper smithing.

As my studies progressed, I was exposed to historic archaeology, the study of archaeological cultures where there are written records. In North America, the historic period begins with the arrival of Europeans and written record keeping. For one of the advanced seminars, I decided to focus on the ruins of a mid-nineteenth century lighthouse built on an island in Lake Michigan not too far from my home in Marinette. Few people knew much about the overgrown brick shell of the lighthouse building on the island. I was able to learn a great deal by tracking down records maintained by the U.S. Lighthouse Service (later absorbed into the U.S. Coast Guard). Amazingly, many of the original logs, purchase orders, and varied other records still existed in the National Archives in Washington, DC. I was able to hire a student there to look up and photocopy these records and send them to me in Madison.

Armed with blueprints, maps, and old photographs, a fellow graduate student and I decided to survey the island in winter when the vegetation was down, to see whether we could locate remnants of the original structures. It turned out, through examination of the documents, that the lighthouse had been built in 1863. Since it was located five miles out from the mainland, the keeper and his family were required to live on this remote island for the navigation season. When we visited the island, we were able to relocate the original tower building, the boat landing, the flag pole standard, the oil house, and of course the outhouse or privy, built of brick. Outhouses are great excavation sites for historic archaeologists. In many cases, you can learn a great deal about a site by excavating an outhouse. Generally, people dispose of many things in the outhouse besides human waste. It is common to find bottles, coins, personal items including jewelry, and sometimes items that people try to hide. After all, who would ever look in the outhouse? Although we were not able to do any excavation at the site, we were able to piece together the physical structures with the historical documents and oral testimony of surviving relatives of the last keepers on the island in the 1930s. This project made me realize just how much information could be gained about past lifeways by combining archaeology, history, and ethnography.

It took a year and a half to complete my master's degree studies. The final step in the process was a day-long exam consisting of two parts. The first part included essay questions on archaeological methods and theory. Questions were written by each archaeology professor in residence, covering topics on radiocarbon dating, stratigraphy, excavation, and classification of archaeological materials and cultures. The second part of the exam consisted of questions on the archaeology of various areas of the world and on big topics such as the origins of agriculture and civilization. The exams were graded anonymously by each professor in the department. I studied for several weeks and often held study-group sessions at my apartment with the other graduate students. The outcome of these exams was used to decide who would get to go on to study for a doctorate degree (Ph.D.). Some students would only receive a master's pass that meant they could go no further in their studies of archaeology at UW-Madison. I was not sure how well I had done; I hoped for the best and anxiously awaited the results when my wife and I visited my parents for winter break. When we returned to Madison, there was a message on the answering machine from my major professor, Dr. Stoltman, stating I had passed, was admitted into the Ph.D. program, and should come and talk to him as soon as possible.

I well remember going in to meet with Dr. Stoltman. He told me that he knew I was still interested in going to law school but hoped that I would consider completing a Ph.D. in anthropology/archaeology at UW-Madison. He said that if I stayed, I would have an opportunity to work under his supervision on a dissertation research project, and that I would likely have an opportunity to be a teaching assistant in the department. I went home immediately and discussed this with my wife Teresa and then my parents. I concluded that I thoroughly enjoyed archaeology and wanted very much to teach at the university level and conduct my own research. So, I decided to enroll in the Ph.D. program, realizing that this probably would require me to complete another four to five years of school on top of the five and half years I had already put in obtaining my BS and MA degrees.

Only a handful of the original twelve students with whom I started went on to work on Ph.D.s. We were required to take several additional seminars focusing on research methods and to choose a minor outside the department. I chose geography because it was closely related to archaeology and required me to take courses in landscape formation, soils, and mapping, all useful areas for an archaeologist. These enhanced one of the most exciting courses I took, a field seminar in Paleoindian archaeology. "Paleoindians" were the Ice-Age hunter-gatherers who were the very first people in North America, 13,000 to 10,000 years ago. The course's classroom component required students to put together a research summary on one of the classic Paleoindian sites on the Great Plains.

The field component of this course took us on a two-week trek to more than a dozen of these sites, from Texas to Colorado. We visited Folsom in New Mexico, where in the late 1920s scientists discovered the first conclusive evidence that American Indians hunted a giant Ice-Age bison species that is now extinct. We also went to Blackwater Draw near Clovis, New Mexico, where archaeologists first identified the Clovis cultural style dating around 12,000 years ago, the oldest pan-North American type of artifact recognized. At Blackwater Draw, excavations revealed a soil layer containing flaked stone projectile points in the midst of mammoth remains. Other sites we visited included some that were massive beds of butchered bones of Ice Age mammals associated with stone weapons and tools. It was a thrill to see these places, many of which I had read about since I was a child, and to see firsthand the topography, climate, and setting of the finds. You can read about a place and artifacts found there, but there is no substitute for being at the actual site, examining data directly!

Prehistoric American Indians first populated Wisconsin and Michigan at least 11,500 years ago. The first people arrived in the western Great Lakes during the end of the Pleistocene Epoch (last Ice Age). As glaciers receded north, new territories opened up for habitation. Small groups of hunter-gatherer extended families began to settle into this new landscape as early as 7500 BC. Archaeologists refer to these post–Ice Age hunter-gatherer cultures collectively as the Archaic Tradition. They made a living by exploiting a wide variety of terrestrial game, migratory waterfowl, fish, and plants. The Archaic Tradition spanned a time of approximately 7500–1000 BC in this part of the Midwest.

DISSERTATION RESEARCH ON OLD COPPER

Great Lakes Archaic Indians were the first to experiment with metal fabrication technologies in North America. Ninety-nine percent pure copper was discovered in the Lake Superior basin in vein form and in the form of nuggets in glacial outwash gravel beds. Through experimentation, Archaic peoples learned to hot- and cold-hammer the copper to produce a variety of projectile points, woodworking tools, harpoons, fishhooks, and jewelry. Many of these tools were used for everyday subsistence activities; however, some copper goods were traded to cultures outside of the region in order to obtain exotic materials, including marine shell and volcanic glass. Archaeologists have referred to these first copper-using peoples as the Old Copper Culture or Industry.

At the time I was in graduate school in the 1990s, little was known about Old Copper societies. Thousands of their artifacts had been found on the surface in Wisconsin and Michigan, and a handful of their cemeteries had been excavated in the 1940s, 1950s, and 1960s by professional archaeologists. The burial sites spanned a very long period of time: 4000–500 BC. The core of the anthropology Ph.D. program at Madison includes an independent research project resulting in a professional-quality dissertation conforming to the university's standards. I started thinking about what I would like to work on for my research, and I became particularly interested in the use of copper by prehistoric native peoples of the western Great Lakes. Two cemeteries from northeast Wisconsin, where I grew up, were from opposite ends of the Old Copper time spectrum. Excavations at the Oconto site had produced burials of just over fifty people. Oconto was thought to date somewhere between 5500 and 3000 BC. The second site, the Riverside Cemetery, was located approximately 30 miles to the north along the border of Wisconsin and

Michigan. Excavations at that site yielded the burials of approximately 75 people believed to date approximately 1000–400 BC. Both sites, incidentally, had been excavated to save the burials from destruction.

I wanted to see what could be learned by comparing these two cemeteries to see what types of grave offerings were present, hoping to learn something about the social organization of these two societies. I was also interested in learning about the trade and exchange in which these two populations participated, many centuries apart. I prepared a research proposal about twenty pages in length and defended it in front of a committee of my professors at UW-Madison. They agreed that it was a worthwhile project and that I should start on it immediately for my Ph.D. research.

My first step was to examine all of the original collections from the two sites that were housed at several museums and universities. This took me to the University of Michigan, the Milwaukee Public Museum, the Oshkosh Public Museum, and a small local museum in Oconto, Wisconsin. This was exciting work! I went through all of the skeletal material. Fortunately, the majority of the skeletons had been sexed and aged by previous researchers including a human osteologist (a biological anthropologist who specializes in human bone identification). I then analyzed all of the artifacts associated with the various burials at the two sites. This involved classifying artifacts into categories of tools, ornaments, exotic materials, and so on. I also weighed all of the artifacts so that I could compare burials by how much copper was included in their graves.

Part of the research involved redating the two sites using more modern radiocarbon dating methods. When the original dates were run back in the 1950s and 1960s, wood charcoal was the most common material dated. It was, of course, always possible that the charcoal was older than the human occupation at the site. The prehistoric inhabitants could have burned very old tree trunks in their campfires, making the dates older than the time the people made the fire. I wanted to find better materials to date and to use newer dating methods that were considerably more accurate. In going through the collections, I came across fragments of textile, bark containers, and even pieces of woven cordage or string. These materials were preserved because they were buried in close proximity or in contact with copper artifacts. When copper weathers, it produces a green oxide; this tends to preserve organic materials. (In fact, today copper salts are used for treating lumber to make it resistant to decay.) From the dates I obtained from these materials, I was able to conclude that the Oconto site burials dated to between 4000 and 3000 BC and that the Riverside burials dated to between 1000 and 400 BC.

I was also able to examine the distribution of artifacts in relation to age and sex at the two sites. The older Oconto site had primarily tools made of local materials buried with the dead. Similar artifacts appeared to be buried with both sexes and a variety of age groups. Therefore, the Oconto burial pattern suggested that the society was an egalitarian hunter-gatherer culture, a society where there is no formalized leadership or pronounced differences in social inequality. Egalitarian societies tend to be small-scale cultures that make a living by hunting and gathering as compared to societies who obtain food via gardening or intensive agriculture. Since there is little opportunity to acquire surplus goods in this type of subsistence economy, there is generally an absence of accumulated wealth. There may be divisions in labor along the lines of sex (male and female roles), but there are usually no formalized leadership positions in hunter-gatherer egalitarian cultures. We know a fair amount about egalitarian societies from information obtained by cultural anthropologists who have studied similar living cultures over the last 100 years.

In sharp contrast, I found that the burials from the Riverside cemetery had pronounced differences in the amount of goods buried with individuals and groups of individuals. At Riverside, just over half of the total weight of the copper artifacts was in the form of beads. Additionally, there were large caches of exotic materials including knives and spear points made from materials that came from hundreds and in some cases thousands of miles away. Most notable was a block of obsidian (volcanic glass) that came from the Yellowstone, Wyoming, area. In comparison to Oconto, the later Riverside people participated in long-distance trade and traded for prestige items that may have been used to convey the status of either individuals or family kin-groups. It was also startling to discover that much of this wealth was placed with young adult women and children. Although it is difficult to know for certain what this pattern represents, it is clear that this society was not an egalitarian society. There were clear differences in the way people were treated at the time of death; this suggests that some individuals and kin-groups had differential access to power, prestige, and wealth. I also believe that the elaborate female and child burials are likely to represent the importance of reproduction in this society. It is possible that some of the wealth reflects arranged marriages between higher-status families.

I was able to present the results of my research at a number of regional and national archaeology conferences, as well as publish in several journals (Pleger 2000, 2001). This is one of the most rewarding aspects of archaeology, the realization that you are contributing to new knowledge and a new understanding of the past. It is the hope of all professional archaeologists that their work will be built upon by future researchers.

PROFESSIONAL LIFE

Besides enjoying research, I knew that I wanted to teach at the university level. While at UW-Madison, I was a teaching assistant and later an instructor in the Department of Anthropology. From there, I went back to UW-La Crosse to teach for four years and to continue to do field work. I was able to spend time in both the classroom and the field conducting archaeological research required under cultural resource management regulations.

In 1998, I left UW-La Crosse to begin a teaching career at UW-Fox Valley in northeast Wisconsin. UW-Fox Valley is a two-year campus of the University of Wisconsin System. It is a small liberal arts college with approximately 1800 students and class sizes that are generally under 35 students per section. I have been at UW-Fox ever since and found it to be a rewarding place to work, as both an archaeologist and a professor. I get to know all the anthropology majors by name and know something about their interests and backgrounds. Many of my students have continued on in archaeology and anthropology at a number of the larger UW campuses. I continue to teach courses in Wisconsin archaeology, North American archaeology, world prehistory, North American Indians, human osteology, and the archaeology field school. The field school allows me to take a select group of students every other summer to work on an actual excavation. I have taught field schools in northeast Wisconsin on a variety of prehistoric Indian sites ranging from a thousand years old to sites dating to the arrival of Europeans in the region in the mid-seventeenth century.

Some of my field research has been the direct result of contributions made by avocational archaeologists or laypeople. For example, a

Clockwise, from top left:

—An early Paleo-Indian Clovis-like fluted point from northeast Wisconsin. This point was brought into UW-Fox Valley by a student for identification. Age is estimated at 12,000-11,000 years old. Photo: Thomas Pleger.

—Samples of Old Copper industry tools from the Western Great Lakes, including projectile points, knives, gaff hook, and axe (upper right). These tools date to approximately 6000–3000 years ago. Lawrence University Collections, Appleton, Wisconsin. Photo: Thomas Pleger.

—UW Colleges 2003 archaeology field school, excavating test units with complex stratigraphy at the Stephenson Island site in Marinette, Wisconsin. Photo: Thomas Pleger.

—Dr. James Stoltman photographing 1992 UW-Madison excavations of a stratified multicomponent Woodland site near Prairie du Chien, Wisconsin. Photo: Thomas Pleger.

—Appleton West High School anthropology teacher Amy Loritz and students sorting garbage for a nutrition assessment research project. Photo: Thomas Pleger.

—Students from University of Wisconsin Colleges excavating a possible Middle Woodland (AD 300–400) prehistoric fire hearth feature in Marinette, Wisconsin. Photo: Thomas Pleger.

—Thomas Pleger explains a profile showing stratigraphy at the UW Colleges 2006 excavations at the Schaefer Farms sites near Whitehall, Trempealeau County, Wisconsin. Photo: Janet Speth.

GARFIELD

student from UW-Marinette contacted me because he had found a copper spearhead while metal detecting on an island in the Menominee River in northeast Wisconsin. He e-mailed me several images and I knew right away that it was a 5000- to 3000-year-old weapon made by Old Copper Archaic Indians. The irony in this find is that it was discovered just outside the present-day Marinette County Historical Society Museum on an island in the Menominee River. Once I knew the approximate location of the find, I was able to look up whether other archaeologists had reported a site there in the past. It turned out that the first state archaeologist had recorded a site in the same location in the 1920s. This piqued my interest; could there still be an archaeological site on the island that was worth investigating? In 2003, I took a group of students there to conduct excavations. Our goal was to try to see if there were more materials associated with the copper spearhead found earlier. Additionally, we wanted to know if there were intact prehistoric deposits. Our excavations revealed several layers of fill, including one layer that produced mixed prehistoric and historic artifacts. We continued to excavate down to the original pre-European surface on the island. From our work, we were able to determine that the copper spearhead came from a disturbed layer that was likely trucked in for modern construction. Although we were not able to relocate the archaeological deposits that were first reported in the 1920s, we could conclude that there were no important materials near the surface.

One of the exciting aspects of being an archaeologist is that you never know what will be the next thing to walk through the door. Avocational archaeologists are the eyes and ears for professionals in terms of finding sites. They are the folks who bring important discoveries to our attention. When someone calls saying they have an artifact for me to look at, I never know if it will be something important or something that is not an artifact at all. People are always surprised when I tell them that the unusual hole in the rock that they are showing me is likely the result of natural rather than human processes. People are also shocked when they come in with a truly ancient artifact. Not too long ago, one of our students came in with a Clovis point that was found at her boyfriend's home during construction. The first people to explore the New World approximately 12,000 years ago used this particular type of flaked stone weapon. Clovis points have been found on the Great Plains embedded in mammoth skeletons. We hope to explore this site in the near future.

For my 2006 field school, UW-Fox archaeologist Janet Speth and I took eight students to Trempealeau County in northwestern Wisconsin, to work on a prehistoric habitation site located on a farm near the town of Whitehall, Wisconsin. This farm is owned by my in-laws, Teresa's parents, and their family has cultivated it for more than a hundred years. Over that time, they accumulated a small collection of stone tools, projectile points, and other artifacts found on the surfaces of their plowed fields. The first time I visited my future in-laws' farm, as an undergraduate dating Teresa, her parents showed me this collection of artifacts. Immediately recognizing some of the artifacts as examples of Paleoindian and Archaic Indian styles, I photographed them and reported them and the locations of the sites to the regional archaeologist at La Crosse. Through the years, I looked for an opportunity to survey and excavate at the farm to determine whether it had intact undisturbed remains below the plowed surface zone.

In 2006, we began the field school by surface-surveying the plowed fields, walking the furrows looking for artifacts. We identified concentrations of stone tools and lithic debris in several fields. The students then set up a grid across the site, using a surveyor's transit. Under the grid, we excavated a series of 2 × 2-meter test units to see what lay under the plow zone. Happily, intact archaeological deposits in stratigraphic order were revealed. Two Woodland Tradition occupations dated within the last 2500 years; we identified these cultural traditions through their pottery and stone blade styles. Beneath these, we found Archaic style flaked stone tools suggesting an age of 3000 to 1500 BC. Beneath that was flaked stone tool-making debris probably dating to Late Paleoindian, 7000–6000 BC, to judge from the two Late Paleoindian projectile points recovered from the site.

Our field school students, coming from several universities including UW-Fox, worked ten-hour days and camped in a nearby park. They learned how to survey, test, excavate, and process artifacts in the field. And they got to know each other pretty well, and to get along cheerfully. Of all the courses I teach, I find field schools most interesting and most rewarding, both in watching students benefit and in discovering new data. We will return to work at the sites on my in-laws' farm, preserved through their careful husbandry of the land.

One of my more unusual projects was one on nutrition assessment research involving one of our local public schools in northeast Wisconsin. (The project was similar to William Rathje's "garbology" research, discussed in our chapter 7.) In 2005, I was approached by a school board member who was interested in testing the effectiveness of their new policies designed to create a more nutritious environment in their schools. These policies included new curriculum in nutrition and overall health, the elimination of junk foods from campus vending machines, and the development of a more healthy hot-lunch program. The idea grew out of a project that the local high school anthropology teacher, Ms. Amy Loritz, was doing. She was using modern-day garbage to teach her students about how archaeologists sorted and interpreted material culture. We were asked if it would be possible to use "garbology" to see if the policies were making a difference. In other words, we were asked to develop a research study that would analyze garbage from one of the high school's lunch periods in order to understand patterns of student eating in relation to nutrition, and whether these data could be used to gauge the success of the school's policies.

Amy and I then pulled in an additional anthropologist, Janet Speth, and a sociologist, Greg Peter from UW-Fox Valley, as well as a nutritional anthropologist from Lawrence University, Mark Jenike, who became the "principal investigator" (the senior project leader). Students from Appleton West High School, UW-Fox Valley (led by undergraduate anthropology student Carol Tanner), and Lawrence University collected and analyzed the data. Together, we developed a three-pronged approach to this research problem: The archaeologists focused on collecting and analyzing garbage; the nutritional anthropology team collected data on what students reported they were eating, measured the students' height and weight, and investigated cultural ideas about food; and the sociology group collected information on how students learned about nutritious and healthy food.

The archaeology component of the project was very unusual. Instead of stone tools and pottery sherds, the students collected food wrappers, containers, and wasted food. Our sampling strategy was to collect garbage data from the lunchroom on four separate occasions throughout the year. The students then separated food waste from on-site food purchases, brought-in food, and food that was purchased off-site. We looked at which types of foods were most frequently wasted. We were able to document that large quantities of fruits and vegetables were wasted, while nearly all high-sugar foods and snacks were consumed. The archaeological data combined with the nutritional anthropology and sociology data showed that although the school's policies were having an impact on student health and nutrition, there was room for improvement. This type of project is a good example of how archaeology can be used to answer modern research questions.

So far, it has been an exciting career! Archaeology is never boring, and people are always excited to hear what you have been working on and what your opinion is of a new discovery or interpretation about the past. The profession stimulates travel; teaching courses on North American and worldwide prehistory, I try to take a trip to important archaeological sites outside my region at least once a year. I've taken community outreach students to Belize to learn directly about Maya archaeology, I've gone by motorcycle to the American Southwest Four Corners region to see Ancestral Puebloan ruins, and flown to Peru to tour classic Inca locales including Machu Picchu. Such in-person experiences enhance my understanding of the worlds of the past and enliven my teaching.

Working as a college professor, you can see your impact upon the futures of your students. Many of my students did not even know what anthropology and archaeology were before taking my courses. Additionally, being a college professor is one way to be a college student forever: you are always learning, growing and pursuing new research, and you have a captive audience with whom to share your enthusiasm.

Talking Points

- Schools seldom encourage youngsters to consider careers in archaeology. Tom Pleger describes how gradual and hesitant his choice of career was, in spite of his strong interest in archaeology since childhood. Should schools program more exposure to archaeology?
- Tom's dissertation research did not involve him in excavation. Using curated collections from salvage excavations conducted by an earlier generation, he brought contemporary technical aids such as radiocarbon dating and stone raw-material sourcing to draw out new knowledge. Turning to stored collections rather than making new, and inevitably destructive, excavations is a dimension of stewardship over our cultural resources.
- What skills and personal traits are necessary to become a successful professional archaeologist?
- Tom's participation in the project to improve school children's diet shows how archaeology can be used to analyze present-day culture. Can you suggest other projects that could use an archaeologist's skills and critical thinking?

Chapter Six

Controversies in Archaeology

Scientists may agree that certain observations constitute significant data, yet may not come to the same conclusion on interpretation. Sometimes, disagreements arise over what phenomena ought to be observed, recorded, and analyzed. We may laugh at medieval farmers' belief that Paleolithic stone axes are thunderbolts, but as Kehoe noted (chapter 4), when a highly-placed administrator of archaeology sees "mammiform" in a little carved pendant and his underlings are afraid to tell him he's got the artifact backward, error can become dogma. Controversies can sprout through an archaeologist's lack of experience with non-Western cultures (that's why archaeologists must study anthropology) or through naïve acceptance of what older generations of professors taught—or the opposite, ambition-driven challenge to everything older archaeologists did. Archaeological data are generally ambiguous insofar as their social meaning, and often their functions as well. Theories are built on selected premises, not always well grounded, and they link to corollaries that may have been overlooked. There are also controversies that are hyped just to sell books. And there are the "Controversies That Never Die"—what we call "zombie science."

We'll start with the zombies. Atlantis is a good example. A television producer remarked that when a film with "Atlantis" in the title shows on the Discovery Channel, fourteen million people tune in. Name the film *Visits to Hissarlik, San Lorenzo, and Tiwanaku*, and nobody looks. So that producer made a very nice video, with good archaeologists working at those sites describing their importance in world history, then stuck on as the title, *In Search of Atlantis*. Your author, Kehoe, appears in the video explaining that pre-Columbian transoceanic voyages were possible and probable, but that alone doesn't make it likely that a lost civilization disappeared into the ocean. Among the fourteen million people tuning in the video were several who took the trouble to find Kehoe's address and send her their theories about Atlantis or other "lost races." One fellow mailed a self-published thick book claiming an ancient race wore extremely tight belts to keep their stomachs small, by which they endured long ocean crossings without any food to populate the New World. Another sent a long scenario ending with the lost-race kings building Atlantis on the grounds of the Hot Springs, Arkansas, Country Club—he enclosed a U.S.G.S. topographic map marked to point out buried walls. We haven't tested the site but are willing to bet that those are golf course embankments, not 11,000-year-old ruins. No use telling these earnest souls that scholars knowledgeable about Plato, author of the story of Atlantis, agree that the story is a parable, a tale made up to teach a moral. Lost continents never die.

Zombie archaeology loves White Gods. Quetzalcoatl is a favorite—not the real Mesoamerican prince, probably twelfth century AD, described in native histories, nor the deity pictured as a huge rattlesnake with plumes or wings, but a fair-haired Viking type carrying civilization to the benighted heathens before sailing off into the sunrise. Or the White God may be called by a Polynesian name, because he sailed around the world carrying civilization through the Pacific. He might be Ancient Egyptian or Libyan or Phoenician or Chinese, or from another galaxy. One nineteenth-century twist on the plot had a Maya princess, Móo, sailing to Egypt to found its civilization. This idea was invented by an intrepid woman explorer, a pioneer photographer wearing a pistol in her belt as she set up her glass-plate-negative camera; her photographs are priceless records of Maya buildings before excavations and restorations, but her Princess Móo unfortunately gives her a bad reputation. The problem with the White Gods and fleeing princesses is that the archaeological record is a history of artifacts, not personalities. Where there are texts to go with archaeological material, they are seldom definitive: Witness the controversies over whether Homer's *Iliad* is historically valid, and the consensus among Maya researchers that although we can now read most of the hieroglyphs on Maya monuments, most were inscribed to glorify the royal patron rather than as cold, factual accounts.

There is a limbo-land where sincere, intelligent people meet zombie archaeologists. Rock art lies in this area, a field where scientific archaeologists' hesitancy lets zombies sneak in. A professor of marine biology in New England announced discoveries of hundreds of rock inscriptions in nearly-forgotten alphabets, from Maine to Utah. He had a remarkable eye for discerning these, undermined by the conceit that he could easily translate them. After noticing too many slips between limited data and grand interpretations, a number of scientifically trained followers slipped away. Many professional archaeologists they consulted pooh-poohed the possibility of foreign writing, or any Old World contacts, in pre-Columbian America. Such dogmatic rejection doesn't sit well with experienced scientists. A couple of these, engineers, asked why one alleged hoax, a stone in northern Minnesota with a long inscription in Norse runes, had not been scanned by high-tech microscope to determine whether the inscription was weathered, as it would be if its date of AD 1362 is valid. They arranged to have this done, and the results support authenticity for the carving. Pre-Columbian transoceanic contacts lie in the limbo between mainstream American archaeology and enthusiasts ready to credit nefarious conspiracies against Truth.

Another line of zombie archaeology intrudes on rock art research. Since Classical Greece, two thousand years ago, and probably earlier, civilized intellectuals have supposed that far-away, exotically dressed barbarians retain pure spiritual knowledge lost to city-dwellers. After Columbus, American Indians filled the bill for "primitive religion." Romantics ignored American First Nations' real histories, believing that because Indians sat on the ground, they were close to primal Mother Earth. Partly through a self-proclaimed historian of religion who couldn't be bothered checking facts, we still have the zombie notion that "shamans" in "primitive societies" practice humankind's earliest religion, unchanged since the Paleolithic. One enthusiast applied the notion to rock art, announcing it has been created by "shamans" coming out of "ecstatic trance" (this from the untrustworthy historian of religion's book). We try to explain that "shamans" are practitioners of historic North Asian religions, whose beliefs and rituals differ thoroughly from those of indigenous religious leaders in Latin America, Australia, and Africa. Dramatized soul journeys performed by North Asian shamans on behalf of people in their communities are not what psychologists term "trance." Creating rock art is not the regular practice of North Asian shamans. Sadly, a few reputable archaeologists bought the zombie theory, declaring they now have the code to European Upper Paleolithic cave art, South African rock art, Western North American rock art, even graffiti on walls of an ancient Maya plaza. Shamans all! Please, people, we say: Scientific archaeology, because it is science, must define its terms precisely and concretely—you mustn't say "shaman" when you refer to practitioners of very different religions. Please, we say, the premise that European Paleolithic religion has persisted unchanged among non-Western nations (not in Europe?) is contrary to anthropologists' knowledge of religions around the world.

We can offer examples of sound archaeological research on rock art. The Society for American Archaeology awarded its 2005 prize for best scholarly book of the year to Kelley Hays-Gilpin for her *Ambiguous Images*, drawing on her discussions with Hopi and Navajo near her university in northern Arizona, detailed examination of ethnographic

—*Top left:* The so-called "Baseball Man," from a rockshelter on the San Juan River in southeastern Utah. The image is actually that of a shield superimposed over a human figure from an earlier time period. Photo: Kelley Hays-Gilpin.
—(*Top right and bottom left*) Sections of Newspaper Rock (near Monticello, Utah), a petroglyph panel with symbols etched in sandstone representing the Fremont, Anasazi, and Navajo cultures. The exact meaning of the symbols is still not clearly understood.
—(*Center*) The Great Gallery, Canyonlands National Park, Horseshoe Canyon. Some of the figures at this site are over 12 feet tall. The largest in this photo is known as the "Holy Ghost" because of its strange hollow eyes and skull-like head. These figures date from the Late Archaic Period (about 2000–1000 BC).
—*(Bottom right)* A hunter spears a deer or antelope in this Early Archaic petroglyph from eastern Wyoming. Photo: Linea Sundstrom.

records, and much fieldwork with avocational as well as with other professional archaeologists. Hays-Gilpin seriously considers the popular shamans-did-it explanation, indicating its lack of fit with both the rock art images she recorded and the First Nations people she consults. Runner-up to Hays-Gilpin's book for the Society of American Archaeology's 2005 award was Linéa Sundstrom's *Storied Stone*. Sundstrom, a CRM archaeologist, grew up in the Black Hills of South Dakota, in country claimed by the Lakota. Like Hays-Gilpin, she focuses on rock art in the region she knows intimately, and develops her interpretations through serious discussions with Lakota friends as well as ethnographic and ethnohistorical records. Like Hays-Gilpin, Sundstrom concludes that the shamans-in-trance explanation does not fit either the variety of pictures she recorded, nor Lakota opinions. Instead of a one-size-fits-all zombie persisting among Western intellectuals for more than two thousand years, Sundstrom offers clear links between rock images in Lakota territory and Lakota mythology and history. It won't explain European Paleolithic art, on another continent and twenty or thirty thousand years earlier.

CONTROVERSIES IN ARCHAEOLOGICAL THEORY

Archaeologists depend on the context of finds for clues to interpretation. A round discoloration in the soil may be a posthole if there is a pattern of such stains resembling the framework for a house, or a scaffold for drying meat or fish if there are only four stains, or a platform if stains are spaced suitably for a wider raised structure. Packed earth might indicate a temple floor if items suggesting worship, but little ordinary debris, lies on it; conversely, hearths with stone knife blades and choppers, bits of food refuse, potsherds, and occasional simple beads can lead an archaeologist to infer that the context of the finds indicates a home.

Some archaeologists assume it's normally going to be straightforward, "cookbook science" following a standard procedure: If it's shaped like an arrowhead, call it "projectile point." If we find it near the hearth with sherds and food remnants, we should look closely at the artifact: If one edge is thin and sharp and the opposite long edge slightly dulled, like the blade of my own kitchen knife, the *context* clues us to postulate a stone knife, not a projectile point, and careful examination points to that interpretation. Furthermore, rather than hinting at a man's presence, the context makes it likely a woman was here, preparing meals. Meticulous attention to artifact details and context should be routine, but there are some people oblivious to the purpose of doing archaeology—recovering the residue of human life from the buried past.

"Cookbook science" archaeology gets controversial when a more scrupulous analysis conflicts with the standard interpretation. This is occurring with claims for evidence of warfare in several regions of prehistoric North America. It should hardly surprise anyone, yet the standard line was that American Indian populations were small and content with their territories. Pueblos, in particular, were called "peaceful," presumably because they never fought U.S. troops. They did fight Spanish invaders, in 1680, in a real war. Evidence for prehistoric warfare between pueblos cropped up again and again, from the difficult but highly defensible building of villages in cliff clefts in Mesa Verde, through hacked-up skeletons, to burned houses with decapitated skulls thrown inside. In several instances, skeletons had been partially butchered like animals. A biological anthropologist who published a broad study of these data, a few indicating processing as if for meat—cannibalism!—brought the controversy over warfare to high heat. No matter how clear the evidence, some Southwestern archaeologists clung to the myth they'd been taught, that prehistoric populations were small, self-contained, nonaggressive. The myth blinded them to the ancient reality that prehistoric Americans had histories quite similar to those of Old World nations.

How much to trust First Nations' oral recounted histories is a related controversy. Southwestern nations, both Pueblos and the 'O'odham in southern Arizona, tell of migrations and wars that appear congruent with various archaeological data. Archaeologists employed by First Nations, or consulting with them, proffer these data buttressing the oral traditions. Controversy rises when, as is usually the case, data could fit more than one legend. Conservative archaeologists conclude that orally transmitted tales are inherently unreliable, their promise of fleshing out dry archaeological data no more than pie-in-the-sky. More liberal archaeologists want to take it case by case, bowing out when it comes to ancestors descending from the sky while accepting accounts presenting series of landmarks that correlate with recognized pottery types radiocarbon dated to the appropriate time.

In between are traditions with less specific material aspects. Osage ritual texts recorded from priests around 1900, within a generation of U.S. conquest of this Midwest Indian nation, have several passages that could be describing Cahokia; the Osage could be descendants of Cahokia, on the edge of their historic territory; the Osage holy texts could explain a figurine found in a Cahokian temple, could explain the gross human sacrifices in the mound south of the Great Plaza, could tell us that the towering mounds represented mighty thunderclouds storming into the city—*if* Osage migration legends refer to the Mississippi-Missouri confluence, *if* knowledge of these holy matters could pass from priest to priest over seven centuries. Is it possible? Conservatives say no, not without writing; liberals point to the mnemonic aids embedded in the powerful ritual texts. It is chilling to read that a priest hesitated to dictate texts to the young Omaha anthropologist (Omaha are closely related to Osage) because the power in the rituals could be deadly to someone not properly taught. The young man's father, a prominent Omaha leader, was in the room and volunteered to take responsibility upon his own shoulders, should the danger be activated. Two weeks later, the father lay dead in that very room. It does make one ponder the possibility that such fearful ritual knowledge passed through so many generations, each rigorously trained to transmit it.

The nature of human nature is a topic forever generating controversy. Among archaeologists, the topic sometimes is tagged "diffusion versus psychic unity." Were inventions made only once in human history, then passed from group to group, "diffusing" through societies? Or are we genetically programmed to figure out a repertoire of inventions? For example, was agriculture invented once, perhaps in the Near East around 11,000 years ago, and the idea and practices of growing crops spread around the world? On the "diffusion" side, we see that agriculture appears in the archaeological record successively later, the farther we get west in Eurasia from the Near East. Particular crops and domesticated animals definitely were taken from earlier locations where the organisms are native, to lands where only humans could have carried them (wheat in western Europe, corn in America north of Mexico). More research, and we get unexpected angles on diffusion: Squash cultivated in Maine several thousand years before corn agriculture reached there, its northern limit; bananas among the first crops in West Africa, a plant originating in Southeast Asia and cultivated there, and in New Guinea, for thousands of years previously! Why were Archaic hunting-fishing communities in Maine growing squash? Did they travel far south into the central Midwest where squash was being grown? Do bananas in West Africa indicate sea trade routes thousands of miles long through the Pacific and Indian Oceans, three thousand years ago?

On the "independent invention" side, all over the world, people assist the growth of favored plants even in environments where field agriculture isn't feasible. The fact that earliest crops in regions distant from the Near East may be local, such as millet in northern China, suggests that as human populations steadily increased over thousands of years, putting greater pressure on wild resources to sustain them, familiarity with useful plants and animals led to experiments with increasing yields, and thereby, agriculture. This is one debate where both sides are right: Our brains stimulated our ancestors to manage food resources, and trade and travels carried domesticated plants and animals far beyond their natural habitats.

Related to the "diffusion versus psychic unity" debate is the controversy over the role of environments in molding human cultures. The "New Archaeologists" favored a perspective termed ecological determinism, that above all, communities adapt to their natural environments. Certainly it is true that no society can ignore its environment: You need warm clothing in Alaska, and it makes sense to rely on fishing if you live on the southern Alaskan coast. How much of cultures are responses to ecological factors, versus interactions with other societies? New Archaeologists liked ecological explanations because ecological factors could be measured and drawn as arrows and boxes in system diagrams, making publications look scientific. Well over a century ago, pioneer anthropologist Franz Boas had submitted evidence that historical factors interact with ecology, even in severe environments such as the Canadian Arctic. Living for a year with Inuit, Boas had been surprised that oral literature, music, and time-consuming ornamentation were important to his hosts. They journeyed for social gatherings and shared necessities with visitors. The basic Inuit outfit of caribou-skin parka, trousers, boots, and mittens is determined, to a considerable degree, by their Arctic ecology, while differences in garment cut are ethnic identifiers, and

Clockwise from top left:

—Inscribed stela at Monte Albán, Mexico (Photo: Alice Kehoe). We can't yet read all the hieroglyphs in this inscription, but they seem to record a king's conquests. Building in background, upper left (see also photo at top right) is a sophisticated astronomical observatory for keeping a ritual calendar. Like the Moose Mountain boulder construction far to the north in Canada, the Monte Albán observatory is approximately two thousand years old.

—Paleolithic carvings of male genitalia, with rings on the back to hang on string. The conventional interpretation, disregarding the suspension rings, has been that they represent a woman's breasts. Roman soldiers liked to hang similar little phallic pendants on their tents and horse gear. (Turn picture at right angle to see "breasts.") Because of the suspension rings carved as part of the pendants, we know they were meant to be viewed as phalli. Photo (Alice Kehoe): from fig. 10 in Jiří Svoboda, 1986, *Mistři damenného dláta*, Panorama, Prague. Drawing (inset) by Alice Kehoe from pendant in Moravian Museum, Brno.

—The Kensington Runestone, unearthed by a farmer in northwestern Minnesota in 1898, is engraved with Norse runes carved in 1362. Could medieval Scandinavians have penetrated deep into mainland North America over a century before Columbus discovered the New World? Photo: Scott Wolter.

—Monte Albán danzante stones were originally considered depictions of dancers (hence the name *danzantes*). A more recent interpretation is that these stones may represent conquered enemies and/or sacrificial victims; many are considered to depict mutilation (note the "scrolls" in the abdominal area, suggestive of evisceration).

—Crew members excavating a butchered mammoth at Dolní Vestonice, Czech Republic. The little carved mammoth-ivory pendants representing male genitalia were found in another section of this site. Photo: Alice Kehoe.

skillfully executed appliqué and embroidery originate from love of beauty and of the family members who will wear the clothing. Ecological determinism would cut human nature out of nature.

Reacting against ecological determinism and efforts to make archaeology look like physics to be scientific, archaeologists have delved into history and into the philosophy of science, and have looked to historians of the philosophy of science to reaffirm our field's goal of understanding humanity. Historical archaeology, the study of the archaeological record of sites with written documentation, has been growing for half a century. Heritage conservation and management (CRM) employs hundreds of archaeologists full time, in addition to project crews and laboratory staff. These archaeologists search archives for property deeds, civil depositions, newspaper stories, and old-timers' memoirs, learning much about personalities and politics. Looking into the founding of Chicago, heritage researchers were startled to see the self-identified "first White trader," Jean Baptiste Pointe DuSable, was African-American; back then, if you were not born to area Indians and you lived and worked in the Euro-American mode, you were White. DuSable resided in a log cabin with his Potawatomi wife; its remains have disappeared, but contemporary cabins with documented Indian residents were usually furnished like Euro-American settlers' homes, containing only a few items from the Indian heritage. The frontier was not a line but a zone partaking of technologies and lifestyles from both sides. Historical archaeology brings out the nuances of the real past that graphs and statistics overlook.

Philosophy of science isn't a subject most people associate with archaeology. Insofar as archaeology is basically a science, albeit one infused with material from the humanities, it is necessary to understand what specialists expect from a science. Following a procedure by rote, "cookbook science," isn't good enough in the long run. Thomas Kuhn, a historian of science, published a concise book in 1962 called *The Structure of Scientific Revolutions*, still a much-cited analysis of how scientists work. Kuhn introduced the term "paradigm" to mean a model of good science in a discipline (borrowing the term from grammar, where it refers to a verb or noun presented as model of conjugation or declension). He claimed that most scientists putter along as their professors taught them, filling in data as if they are jigsaw puzzle pieces, assuming the accumulated data will show a big picture. "Paradigm" would be both the big picture and a model procedure to produce it. Kuhn pointed out that "anomalies" constantly crop up in science, data that "shouldn't" occur if the paradigm model is correct. Eventually, enough people working in the field notice enough anomalies to become uncomfortable, and a "revolution" happens, led by a courageous researcher introducing a new "paradigm" better able to explain all the data. Kuhn's textbook example was the revolution in astronomy when the classical picture of the universe circling around the earth was challenged by Copernicus, Tycho Brahe, and Galileo insisting that picturing the earth circling around our sun accommodates data that had appeared to be anomalous.

Reacting to Kuhn's dramatic image of revolution, another philosopher, Stephen Toulmin, argued that sciences accumulate *and accommodate* new data, modifying the general pictures until, perhaps, someone points out that contemporary science has come to differ rather radically from what had been accepted several generations ago. Toulmin proposed looking at sciences as so many species of investigations, each with marked characteristics at a particular point in time and space, but with descendants that include mutants and that also drop "genes" (ideas) out of the population. Toulmin's "paradigm" was Charles Darwin's model of biological evolution, descent with modification of ancestral type. Thus, Toulmin argued for evolutionary change in science, not static procedures periodically overthrown for new models. Stepping back from the fracas, we can see that Kuhn and Toulmin can both be right: Kuhn in that a normal science (his term) employs mostly puzzle solvers reluctant to upset the cart until it's grabbed by a stronger personality ready to brave the old guard, and Toulmin in that descent with modification is usual in any science, incrementally building a population inclining toward a newer model.

All of this happens in archaeology. During the first half of the twentieth century, researchers fitted data to a model picturing agriculture, pottery, metallurgy, and architecture being invented in the Near East and spreading out to barbarians such as the ancient British. Then, after 1950, we had radiocarbon dating. Instead of guessing or estimating from depth of buried remains, we sent samples of organic matter from a site occupation to a laboratory that counted emissions of radioactive carbon-14 from the sample, calculated how many years had elapsed since the organism had stopped breathing in carbon, and sent back a "date" (approximate probable number of years before 1950).

To the surprise of many, some Western Europe and Middle Eastern sites had innovations earlier than similar ones in the Near East. First reaction was to turn the older paradigm on its head, and see Near Easterners begging barbarians for the new best things. Soberer reflection on the sets of data broke up the simplistic models, whether East-to-West or West-to-East. The spread of wheat agriculture and domesticated cattle, of metallurgy, of architectural technologies and forms, was not a march of civilization but a complicated map of incursions, colonizations, trade systems, empire building and revolts—*multiple* models. The paradigm got really stretched when newer excavations and radiocarbon dating revealed that the earliest pottery occurs in northeastern Asia and Japan (connected at the time), before the Pleistocene Ice Age had ended! It would be several thousand years before pottery appeared in the Near

East. Of course, we now have new questions: Was pottery-making invented in northeastern Asia, then independently in agricultural villages thousands of miles and years away? Or did it spread slowly across the little-researched northern forests of Asia, finally to be taken up, with considerable changes, in the Near East? More surveys, more excavations!

Up close to controversies over models and theories, new ideas look radical and taking them up, revolutionary. Kuhn's image of paradigms overthrown excites passions. Standing back, Toulmin's evolutionary changes seem apparent. There are always commonly accepted mainstream procedures and models, and alternatives favored by fewer practitioners. In the case of whether civilization "marched" out of the Near East, there had always been a few archaeologists arguing that Western Europe developed more independently than the dominant model held. When radiocarbon dating supported their earlier dates in Western Europe, their models became dominant in the population of ideas.

Continuing research produces more data, shifting probabilities among competing explanations. The Kehoes found distinctive small weapon points in a Northwestern Plains bison corral dated approximately AD 200 and saw that these earliest true arrowpoints were made for several centuries, gradually appearing farther south, and then no more. It was reasonable to hypothesize that the style, along with bow-and-arrow weapons and a relatively rare pottery style, indicated movement of Athabascan-speaking hunters out of the Canadian Northwest, onto the Plains rich with bison herds, gradually moving southward until by about AD 1400 they reached the Southwest, to become known as Apache and Navajo. Then, a great deal of exploration for oil and gas in the Canadian Northwest carried with it considerable archaeological exploration as required by heritage protection laws. After a couple of decades of amassing information on the region's prehistory, it became evident that the hypothesized Apachean arrowpoints and pottery style failed to turn up. Where likely ancestors did turn up was to the east, where the prairies meet forests, way off any route between Northern and Southern Athabascan speakers. Were we back to Square One, with no clue as to how Apacheans came to live in the Southwest when all other Athabascan-speaking nations live in the Northwest? No, because the same decades of research brought much more information on prehistory along and to the west of the Rockies, indicating that Apacheans had probably moved south out of the Northern Rockies borderlands about AD 700, filtering into the Southwest a few centuries later. Their readiness to adopt technology from societies among whom they moved makes them indistinct archaeologically, until some of them began constructing their signature round log hogans in the Southwest.

Calls for archaeology to "be a true science," to "have its own independent theory," are trumpeted now and then. Why should we limit explanations to behaviors that anthropologists and historians document for human societies? Isn't it possible that some societies in the past operated differently from any observed living society? Of course it's possible, but we're still not free to stray far from known behaviors. Ursula K. Le Guin, a fantasy and science fiction novelist, is the daughter of famous American anthropologist Alfred L. Kroeber. In an interview, Le Guin said that as a child listening to her parents and their friends, she wondered what a society would be like *if* . . . if reality for some society was beyond anything we have seen historically—an idea that Le Guin's fiction explores. In contrast, as practitioners of a science archaeologists must be able to point to a real example of postulated behavior, or construct a closely reasoned chain from an example to the inferred variant behavior. Archaeology is a historical science, and the historical sciences—geology and paleontology, also—explain the past by relating data from the past to processes observed in the present. Observe rainwater cutting a gully as it runs off a slope, and you can explain the Grand Canyon. Observe a bird's skeleton, and you can infer that the fossil *Archaeopteryx*, with similar skeletal structure, once flew. Observe a rural agricultural village in Jordan, and you can make plausible, scientific interpretations of Neolithic walls and tools. Late Prehistoric Puebloans such as those at Mesa Verde invested much thought and labor in defense, unlike historic Puebloans, *but not unlike any historic human communities*. We heard a Southwestern archaeologist declare, "We must have independent archaeological thinking!" and then in the next breath mention that it was an avocational archaeologist retired from the military who clued him in to the defensive pattern of Late Prehistoric pueblos in their study area.

Controversies in archaeology generally fall into one or another of two types, those claiming professionals refuse to *believe* alleged evidence, and those within the discipline debating what is most significant to interpretation. You will recall from chapter 3 the conversation between the Kehoes and a *National Enquirer* reporter about the Moose Mountain site in Saskatchewan, in which the reporter asked whether the site was a landing pad for extraterrestrial spaceships, as the best-selling author of *Chariots of the Gods* contended. The reporter had no interest in any scientific evidence to the contrary, nor was he concerned that the *Chariots* author had never physically visited the site; he was only interested in the author's account that "His spirit flew over and was at the site . . . and flew back and told him it was for extraterrestrial spaceships."

What could we say to that? We don't believe there is evidence of extraterrestrials landing on Earth? He'd say, "Why won't you *believe* psychic archaeology?" We won't *believe*, because every set of data referred to by the psychic can alternately be explained by reference to observations of behavior carried out by flesh-and-blood humans in the region, either presently or in the recent past. The Kehoes had talked with several Cree people whose nineteenth-century forebears lived around Moose Mountain. These people described how their bands appointed a man to watch sunrise and sunset against horizon landmarks and to use the sun's path to maintain a calendar for his community. These accounts are a model to explain the astronomical lines-of-sight in the boulder structure: we related processes in the present to data from the past and found a strong fit. No one has seen extraterrestrial spaceships in Saskatchewan, nor anything else that will not fit earthbound models.

Within the discipline of archaeology, professionals may debate whether a theory ("paradigm") adequately covers sets of data. When the Kehoes and their astronomer collaborator announced their interpretation of Moose Mountain as a solstice observatory, presumably for calendar-keeping, some colleagues doubted, supposing it could have been a record of a Sun Dance ritual lodge. We'd asked our Cree friends about this, and they explained why it would not fit as marker for a Sun Dance lodge: it lacked certain necessary features, and the rock lines had no relevance to a Sun Dance ritual. As to the criticism that earlier anthropologists recording observations of Saskatchewan First Nations had not noted calendar keepers, our Cree friends said that once their land filled up with Canadian settlers, they got printed calendars and no longer needed to appoint a calendar keeper. Thus, detailed information on recent human behavior in the region adequately explained the archaeological data.

We were able, too, to satisfy a critic wanting an ecological determinant to explain building the boulder structure: widely scattered hunting bands needed to meet periodically to find spouses, trade raw materials and artifacts not available in their locations, and adjudicate disputes between bands. Only in the height of summer, when travel is easy and game abundant, could all the bands gather in a rendezvous of as many as several thousand people. Each band needed to keep a calendar in order to plan their travel so that their rendezvous time was synchronized. Controversy within our discipline over interpretation of this unusual site was resolved through thorough research into processes observed in the present.

Talking Points

- This chapter discusses two quite different types of controversies in archaeology, those outside the profession and fed by romantics and conspiracy theorists convinced that "the media" won't tell the real truth, and controversies within the profession over validity of procedures. The insider controversies raise significant questions over our sources of knowledge and ability to think clearly, not only in regard to archaeological data but for any observations.
- Recall that author Tom Pleger planned to become a lawyer, assuming that with controversies over repatriating human remains and artifacts

to First Nations, along with stricter enforcement of antiquities protection laws, a lawyer with good knowledge of archaeology would be in demand. Controversies he anticipated have not developed to the degree that many expected, due to efforts to maintain goodwill in repatriation requests, and there has not been much challenge to antiquities protection—looters are usually caught red-handed, realizing that they have lost the gamble they have taken.

Chapter Seven

The Future of the Past

Archaeology mines the past. We dig into it and take out of it the residue of life in the past. This is not an infinite resource. Should our generation continue to take, take, take an irreplaceable patrimony? Is it enough that we store what we take in museum back rooms and display the best-looking artifacts to the public?

These questions arise among a heap of issues confronting archaeologists, as well as the public who support us through taxes and fees. How much of what is pulled from the past becomes known through public ownership? We can only guess the quantities illegally looted and sold to private collectors. Does the public good trump private property rights? Should sites be preserved without disturbance, or routinely subjected to limited investigation, or thoroughly excavated and all the field notes and finds curated? What about restoration to enable tourists and schoolchildren to visualize and experience life at that time and place? If restoration is chosen, should structures be rebuilt directly on their footprints, or nearby so as to preserve the actual foundations? What about the Chinese method of preservation—replacing structural parts, such as wooden beams, as needed to keep the appearance of a structure intact for centuries? Is that preservation? Is the replica of Lascaux Cave near the closed-off protected real cave a valid experience for tourists? Is the Mexican government correct in putting ugly pebbles in restored portions of ancient building walls, to make it clear which is the original and which the modern repair?

Stewardship is a word that has come into frequent use as cultural heritage management evolved into its current position as a major business sector. It is important to note that archaeological sites and materials are protected on federal lands and on many state lands. Basically, the issue is conservation of resources. Just as clear-cutting forests leaves nothing for our children, bulldozing landscapes robs our children. Archaeological excavation is destructive—not as blatant and ugly as bulldozing, but it nevertheless deprives the next generation of the opportunity to experience the presence of the past, and to apply new techniques of analysis to increase knowledge of the past. From the standpoint of responsible citizenship, the destruction of landscapes and sites betrays our obligation to protect what has been bequeathed to us, that we may pass it on to our heirs.

Archaeologists should be active in curbing enterprises that would obliterate existing geography. When efforts to persuade against, or modify, developers' plans have not succeeded, then archaeologists are justified in salvaging as much knowledge as possible through excavation. Sites that aren't threatened may be investigated and still preserved for those who will follow us. This ethic of stewardship permits limited excavation to obtain information, in many cases facilitated by technology for noninvasive imaging. A century ago, people were thrilled with pictures of hundreds of workmen hacking at walls, stripping down to floors, exposing many square meters of an ancient city. Today, the most admired picture is of a single smiling person, a farmer or retired local resident, standing on a site that hasn't been hacked into, thanks to the steward's watchful advocacy of preservation.

Stewardship involves the contemporary community, politicians, and descendants of those who lived in the region in times past. Local residents may want subdivisions of expensive homes or shopping malls; politicians may want to increase the tax base or glorify and market to tourists an otherwise insignificant attraction, such as Ronald Reagan's boyhood home. Descendants of First Nations, quite possibly living over a thousand miles distant because the 1830 Indian Removal Act forced their forebears to Oklahoma, may be worried that any construction might disturb the graves of their ancestors. Stewards understand competing claims and wishes. CRM companies have staff to talk with the various stakeholders in a project area, individually and in group meetings. The final outcome may leave everyone disgruntled. The archaeological steward's goal is to raise awareness of the several, diverse interests in a site or locality and persuade against destruction. If persuasion proves futile, it falls to the archaeological steward to salvage as many data as possible before destruction—the result of which cannot be as satisfactory as preserving data *in situ*.

TOURISM

Heritage tourism is growing rapidly. Worldwide, close to 600,000,000 adults travel each year to visit places of historic and cultural interest. With so many millions of couples and families driving for holidays, a stop to see something more interesting than the gas-station restroom is welcome. Governments at every level—national, state, and municipal—promote historic places, fostering employment as well as pride. Archaeology contributes to tourism both by identifying sites and by revealing more of documented historic places than can be retrieved from written records alone. Often, a curious problem arises: *Which* period in the past will be presented?

Most places where people have lived have been occupied for centuries, even millennia. What makes a locality desirable for a home—flat, well drained, near fresh water—usually remains the same over generations. Archaeologists find layer after layer of floors or campsites. For the archaeologist this is great, showing through the successive layers (stratigraphy) how cultures changed through time. For the tourism developer, it's a nuisance. Let us say you're looking at the big Late Prehistoric Mandan Indian town in North Dakota, on a high bluff overlooking the Missouri River, called the Double Ditch Site. Visitors saw dozens and dozens of round bowl-shaped depressions clustered together, and a double ring of ditch surrounding the cluster. Now the archaeologist brings in a crew and imaging equipment. Those bowl-shaped depressions are the remains of sod-covered houses built into round, shallow flat-bottomed holes, built and rebuilt as the wooden frames decayed: Which floor represents "the Mandan house?" Defensive ditches, too, and their adjacent palisades were rebuilt, so that we now can trace at least four ditches. Rebuilding of defenses and houses went on more or less continually as needed, here and there within the defendable bluff-top location. If the State of North Dakota Tourism, or the Mandan Nation (now on a reservation some distance away), want to display the town to tourists, must they exhibit diagrams of the structures overlapping and intruding into earlier occupation phases? If they simply go by the mapping, prior to archaeological excavations, of an apparently double ditch and cluster of house ruins, are they misleading the public and the contemporary Mandan people?

Sometimes the issue isn't discussed. When Mexico City added more subway tunnel downtown, construction excavation went through the impressive Aztec Templo Mayor (Main Temple), uncovering spectacular sculptures and offerings, some taken by the Aztec themselves from much more ancient temples. The tourism authority exposed the Templo Mayor for a permanent attraction. Underneath are layers from predecessors of the Aztecs that no one but archaeologists knows about. Artifacts and records of what was observed as the subway tunnel was cut are in museum storerooms. Even if the authorities had decided to display the more ancient ruins—for example, the way Jorvik Viking Center is accessible to tourists in an underground level beneath a shopping plaza in York, England—it would not have been feasible to display

Clockwise from top left:
—Statues on the steps of Templo Mayor, in the Aztecs' capital city Tenochtitlán (now Mexico City).
—Sipán, Peru, adobe-brick tomb of a Moche ruler, early first millennium AD. Tourists flock to see the ruler's gold and sacrificed retainers, including a guard (upper left) and a dog. Tourism to such archaeological sites is important to local economies.
—Teotihuacán, Mexico, was the greatest city in the Americas two thousand years ago, comparable to its contemporary city, Rome. Below the pyramids is the main avenue of the city, lined with three-story-high palaces, temples, and administrative buildings. Mexico maintains this central section of the ancient city for tourism.
—Skull Rack at Templo Mayor, Mexico City (Aztec Tenochtitlán). Tourists are fascinated by this large, square platform, believed to have served as a base for stakes on which the decapitated heads of human sacrifices and/or conquered enemies were impaled for display.
—For over 1,100 years the Maya built Tikal, expanding the site until it covered an area of 25 square miles and contained over 60,000 residents. Temple I, the funerary shrine of Jasaw Chan K'awil, was likely constructed between AD 731 and 734. His tomb was discovered at the base of the temple.
—Detail from the Skull Rack at Chichén Itzá.

every time period's stratum. York, after all, destroyed the medieval and early-modern levels between the shopping mall and thousand-year-old Jorvik. What will attract the most tourists? Vikings or a medieval town? Aztecs or "Early Postclassic"? With a large restoration for tourism costing millions of dollars, name recognition and glamour count.

What time period is selected for exhibition may be only one issue in archaeological projects for tourism and public education. Colonial Williamsburg and plantations nearby had slaves living in cabins, but restoration for visitors at first ignored these humble dwellings. As the civil rights movement of the 1960s fought for respect for African-Americans, a few scholars asked about material evidence for their forebears' way of life. Archaeologists began investigating the localities where records indicated slaves and freed blacks had been housed. We get a gut experience of slavery when we go from the gentry's handsome mansions to the little wooden cabins, often dirt-floored, where slaves slept on straw pallets. Another facet of African-American history comes from archaeology of the cemetery where black New Yorkers were buried in the eighteenth century. Exposed when building the World Trade Center in lower Manhattan (and destroyed when the terrorist planes hit on September 11, 2001), the cemetery, like slaves' cabins on many plantations, revealed persistence of some African traditional practices as well as accommodation to working-class customs of the time.

ARCHAEOLOGY AS ENTERTAINMENT

No, we don't mean spending a Sunday afternoon shoveling out graves, looking for gold. (And getting arrested!) We're thinking of movies, video games, mystery novels, and TV dramas featuring drop-dead-gorgeous forensic archaeologists. We should add documentaries for the Discovery Channel, the History Channel, National Geographic Specials, and—if you can get BBC—a very popular reality-TV series of British archaeologists excavating actual sites. Archaeologists are indeed detectives, and since our investigations do have some tantalizing questions, we can fill quite a number of leisure hours for kids and adults.

Participating in real archaeological projects attracts thousands every year. The U.S. Department of the Interior runs Passport in Time (PIT), bringing volunteers of all ages to crew surveys and excavations in national forests and parks. These projects on public lands are permitted because they are scheduled and closely supervised by federal-government archaeologists; otherwise, *it is illegal to disturb or collect from any public lands.* Crow Canyon in Cortez, Colorado, is a nonprofit business providing year-round instruction and experience on Pueblo sites. Most state and provincial avocational archaeological societies sponsor summer digs, in which qualified professional archaeologists direct the volunteers, and the projects adhere to legal and ethical responsibilities. Scraping dirt with a sharpened trowel for five hot and dusty (or hot and humid and buggy) days may not be everyone's idea of a dream vacation, but the camaraderie is great, and so is the thrill of recognizing a long-hidden piece of someone's life from a time ages ago.

Another popular business is archaeology tours. The Archaeological Institute of America, many museums, university alumni organizations, and cruise and travel agencies offer tours with professional archaeologist lecturers at sites. Tours operated on behalf of nonprofit institutions such as the Archaeological Institute, museums, and alumni usually make the tour a fund-raiser, including a donation as part of the fee. We should mention that one can visit many well-known sites on one's own—and if one does, or books through an ordinary holiday-travel agency, beware of the guides at the site urging you to hire them. Some self-employed guides are knowledgeable and helpful, but others purvey pretty fantastic bull. (Recall the example in chapter 3 of vacationers in Cancún, Mexico, who spent a day at the nearby Maya town of Tulúm and came home persuaded that extraterrestrials had built it.) Whether you go on your own or with a reputable archaeological tour, read up on the site(s) beforehand so you can understand what you're looking at.

Considering the hundreds of archaeology tours and documentaries available at any time, the notion that archaeology is esoteric is obviously untrue. A television producer told us that a video she made for the Discovery Channel, showing Hissarlik (ancient Troy), Tiwanaku in Bolivia (c. AD 1000), and the Olmec city of San Lorenzo (c. 1400 BC) in Mexico, would draw fourteen million viewers from around the world. Many of these may be couch potatoes, yet hundreds of thousands of active tourists are counted each year, even at relatively out-of-the-way and obscure sites such as Montezuma Castle National Monument in Arizona (a prehistoric pueblo with no connection to the Aztec emperor), or Alberta's Head-Smashed-In bison slaughter locality. Think of it: Every year, millions of people choose *not* to spend a day at a shopping mall and instead drive miles into the countryside to walk around ruins! Archaeology means business, in cultural resource management; in the huge tourism industry; and in publishing the broad variety of coffee-table books, videos and DVDs, guidebooks, and mystery novels. The past has a lucrative future.

ARCHAEOLOGICAL SKILLS FOR THE PRESENT

Curious as it seems, archaeologists' skills and data play vital roles in many current hot-button research strategies. Archaeologists have the longest view of human history, stretching from early hominids' crude tool-making, through breakthroughs in inventing ways to survive in temperate and even Arctic climates, to developing agriculture and industrial mass production.

Material Culture

Archaeologists read human history out of the physical remains of human behavior, that is to say, from *material culture*, and this expertise has surprising application to modern needs. For example, archaeologist William Rathje and his students looked through city garbage in Tucson, Arizona, checking actual discards against what interviewed householders said they threw away. Then he extended his research to a cold-weather city, Milwaukee, Wisconsin. In both cities, people interviewed at their front doors underestimated the number of alcoholic beverage bottles and cans in their garbage cans—good citizens didn't want to admit, or perhaps themselves underestimated, how much drinking went on in their homes. Rathje's study interested municipal administrators dealing with garbage collecting and disposal—and the professor who began merely by wondering how American household discards compare with those from prehistoric Maya found himself an internationally known "garbologist." As another example, English archaeologist Daniel Miller interviewed shoppers in London supermarkets about their choices in everyday purchases, thinking that perhaps there would be clues to prehistoric Britons' food choices, and found himself consulted by consumer marketing experts. In both these examples, the archaeologists' orientation toward material culture uniquely illuminates contemporary consumer behavior.

Environmental Assessment

Analyses of data spanning the last two million years reveal climate changes and the human, animal, and plant reactions and adaptations to these changes. Geologists and paleontologists provide related knowledge, while archaeologists focus on how human intelligence managed environmental challenges. Our present debate on global warming requires many contributions from archaeologists: When did human use of fire reach a stage where carbon gases and alterations in plant cover affected the planet's climate? How did human communities cope with the warming climate trend that reached a climax, then ameliorated, four to five thousand years ago? What have been the effects of deforestation?

Archaeologists' research on the "collapse of civilizations"—sometimes only movement from scenes of natural disasters or leached-out fields, sometimes the disintegration of political-economic states—is brought to bear on political scientists' interpretations of current events. To the question of whether our, or every, civilization is doomed to be eclipsed by later societies, archaeologists show that the answer depends on whether you look at material culture or political establishments. The latter seem inevitably to eventually lose out as transportation and warfare technology upsets earlier advantages, while regardless of military or economic factors, styles gradually gain and decline in popularity. A few inventions, such as scissors, are so effective that they've been the same for several thousand years.

Archaeologist Alfred Kroeber, assisted by a young woman colleague, Jane Richardson (Hanks), used his skill in analyzing style shifts in prehistoric American ceramics to chart style cycles in European women's dress; they found hemlines, waists, and necklines rose and fell within definite boundaries for three centuries until, after World War I, skirts became dramatically short and the whole dress radically simpler. We still don't know whether the unimagined horror of the Great War provoked people to reject pre-war ideals, but Kroeber's study does demonstrate correlations between political and economic events and material culture.

Long-Range Planning

Long-range planning obviously needs long-range data. These data should reflect common people's everyday life as well as state rituals, wars, and dynasties. For example, to see that ordinary households change their taste in pottery decoration from generation to generation, often apparently regardless of political stability or change, tells us that cultural traditions have powerful persistence yet inherent capacities to modify. Archaeologists chart cultural patterns and alterations that help us see and assess what has been happening in our time. It is our responsibility to bring these data to our fellow citizens; archaeologists today need to speak up, to become skilled in communicating with the public through work with schools and with journalists, writing in popular style, speaking to local groups and inviting them to visit projects, and contacting legislators.

INDIGENOUS ARCHAEOLOGY AND CONTESTED OWNERSHIPS

Today's maps present results of conquests and migrations that often obscure earlier political formations. European invasions of North America overwhelmed First Nations' ways of life, without, in most cases, extinguishing the nations themselves. Nearly all archaeologists working in North America are, and have been, of European descent and sponsored by Euro-American institutions. Who owns America's pasts? Descendants of the indigenous people who left the data, or representatives of the foreigners who dispossessed them?

From their late-nineteenth-century population nadir (due to epidemics and diseases exacerbated by poverty suffered after destruction of First Nations' economies), American indigenous nations rebounded to reclaim sovereignty over their peoples and resources. Britain's policy of making treaties with American First Nations, implicitly acknowledging their sovereignties, continued under United States and Canadian governments. It follows that since these treaties remain valid, descendants retain inherent sovereignty except where specifically given up or delegated. A century ago, many (but not all!) anthropologists were paid to fill museums with ancient pots, weapons, ritual objects, and skulls. The practice declined as museum storage rooms became crowded, but collections stayed in the cities, separated from their makers' communities.

After World War II, in which thousands of First Nations men served in the armed forces and hundreds of thousands more of their men and women worked in factories and fields to support the war effort, younger indigenous leaders requested the return of objects and skeletons taken from their homelands. Most Americans and Canadians sympathized. The United States Congress passed a law in 1990, the Native American Graves Protection and Repatriation Act (NAGPRA), mandating return of human remains and grave goods to kin, if a connection could be made between the materials and the group making the request. Enforcement of this mandate erupted into legal tangles when the several northwest United States Indian nations, settled on the Colville Reservation, demanded repatriation of the 9,400-year-old man's skeleton recovered when it eroded out of the bank of the Columbia River near Kennewick, Washington. None of the Colville Reservation people could prove that their *actual families* lived around Kennewick nearly ten thousand years ago, and to make the issue more difficult, "Kennewick Man" doesn't look much like historic Columbia River indigenous people. Colville leaders argued that he lived on their ancestral territory and surely wasn't a European; therefore, he was an

American Indian of the Columbia River Valley and belonged in the Colville cemetery, not in a museum somewhere. They said they were affronted by the idea that scientists should study their predecessor in a laboratory.

Biological anthropologists, on the other hand, were eager to secure data on one of the best preserved of the few examples of really early Americans—does he show affiliation with an Eastern Asian population of his time? What changes have occurred in the physical characteristics of indigenous Americans over ten thousand years? No artifacts were recovered accompanying the skeleton (the site was buried under dumped dirt to discourage looting, and it may be that the man had drowned and was never put in a grave). Lawyers argued the case pro and con, year by year, highlighting the ethical obscurities of the NAGPRA law. Canada has recognized indigenous rights to ancestral remains, similarly raising ethical debates but somewhat advantaged by laws placing discoveries of antiquities under Crown (governmental) ownership.

Kennewick Man gets publicity, but peaceful accommodations don't make news. An increasing number of North American First Nations now have their own archaeological programs, hiring both Euro-Americans and their own citizens to conduct research and curate finds. One purpose of these programs can be to document the nation's territory through sites referred to in its oral or written history, or exhibiting its characteristic artifacts and settlement pattern. Another goal may be teaching its history by using artifacts and sites to make it real to their people. Programs usually include young people from the nation on the archaeological crew, motivating them to be stewards of their patrimony and often to pursue more formal education. Their elders act as consultants. Euro-American archaeologists supervising excavations say they found that they, too, gained education, benefiting from indigenous knowledge of the landscape, resources, and details of customary practices.

Indigenous archaeologies—in the plural, to emphasize diversity of views about local pasts—are carried out now in many parts of the world. Maoris in New Zealand, Aborigine Nations in Australia, and Zulu in South Africa are in situations similar to First Nations in Canada and the United States. Their archaeologies, like ours, uncover both the historic colonial past and the fully indigenous past. Along with archaeology of slave quarters on plantations, a brothel near the Capitol in Washington, DC, miners' camps in Colorado, and other sites of working-class lives, indigenous archaeologies reveal much about the larger society in which these people lived alongside the well-to-do. Indigenous archaeologies also are relevant to environmental questions, adding direct data on past environments and their changes, plus interpretations drawn from local cultural knowledge. Our favorite is the Nez Percé man in Idaho who explained that there are hardly any elk left in the mountains because the prairie chickens don't dance anymore. His anthropologist friend thought he might be telling about a myth, until the man pointed out that the territory where prairie chickens used to perform courting dances on the lower grasslands was also elk winter grazing ground. With wheat farms taking over the land, the prairie chickens disappeared and elk were starving over the winters. This isn't, strictly speaking, archaeology, but it illustrates indigenous knowledge that can steer an archaeologist toward insightful interpretation.

* * *

We've described, in this chapter, the many ways that make archaeology meaningful to millions of people. Far from a tiny pastime of Professor PhuddieDuddies, archaeology today is vital to tourism, historical research including environmental sciences, and indigenous nations' claims for justice. Via mystery novels and television dramas, it entertains huge audiences, even those who don't tune into the History and Discovery channels and BBC reality shows. Beyond enjoyment of archaeology is our responsibility for stewarding the irreplaceable heritage from the past. You don't need to participate actively in archaeology to support the conservation of our patrimony so that succeeding generations may carry on research and take pleasure in seeing sites, artifacts, and entertainments testifying to that past.

For a discussion of opportunities and careers in anthropology, as well as a list of UNESCO-recognized, archaeologically researched World Heritage sites in North America, see the Appendix at the end of this book.

Talking Point

- What archaeological sites are in your community's area? (Inquire at your nearest museum or college.) How were they discovered? Historic as well as prehistoric sites count. How are they preserved—or do they need more protection?

Chapter Eight

Archaeology's Realm
The Grand Sweep of Human History

Our chapter title sounds like a blockbuster movie—starring King Tut and Cleopatra, Viking raiders, Crusaders, Christopher Columbus, Thomas Jefferson, Shakespeare, Quetzalcoatl, and *Homo erectus*. Great plot, too: Mild-mannered, geeky grad students morph into sweaty, stripped-down, never-say-die pursuers of the elusive Past. Here it hides in the form of stone flakes, there it transforms into pottery sherds, now again it appears as round dark stains betokening a wooden house, then suddenly it bursts blindingly out as golden goblets around a crowned skeleton. Honestly, we're archaeologists because no other field of inquiry opens up the entire range of human experience, over more than two million years' time and covering the whole planet. Cultural diversity? That's archaeology! Global studies? Yes! Exercise for mind and body? You bet!

Archaeology is absolutely necessary to understand human history, ancient and recent. Archaeology reveals our material lives and a good deal of our spiritual quests. Archaeology serves as checks and balances to documented history. Through archaeology, the common people of the ages come to light, alongside their rulers and priests. Through archaeology, revolutionary inventions come into view surrounded by the social life that fostered them.

Huge as its scope is, archaeology can hold pitfalls (and we mean more than going kerplunk into an excavation trench). It is not for the faint-minded. Critical thinking is the backbone of archaeological interpretation, and scientific method its feet.

CRITICAL THINKING

We humans survived Ice Ages and global warmings, colonizing nearly every corner of land, because we are born with broad capacities for critical thinking. We observe, we classify, we compare, we test. But we are social beings. We learn from each other. That's crucial, to learn to recognize and escape danger. Unhappily, we also learn a lot that isn't true, too often falsehoods that endanger other people. Hitler taught Germans and Austrians that Gypsies, Jews, homosexuals, and developmentally disabled people were about to wreck their society, persuading his followers to murder more than six million men, women, and children imprisoned in camps, not to mention millions more starved or shot on battlefields. Critical thinking grapples with "popular knowledge," what "everybody knows" without questioning.

Hitler, as it happened, liked archaeology. The Nazis ordered archaeological investigations of some sites threatened by building projects, and they supported classification schemes purporting to link Aryans with admired artifacts. Nazi versions of "science" in archaeology weren't horrible like their cold-blooded "medical" experiments, but they do illustrate how prejudice can distort archaeological interpretation. "Popular knowledge" in Nazi Germany sustained its armies by embracing feel-good notions of German superiority and foreign treachery and weakness.

This worst-case scenario of misusing archaeology emphasizes how important it is to look at empirical data—what actually is found and, fully as vital, the context in which it lies. A step beyond looking straight at actual data is the linkage of data to interpretation, the chain of signification. Somebody with no experience in archaeology, like a Montana rancher we met, might pick up pottery sherds and think they were dried-up orange peels. End-of-story for him, until we explained that he was holding evidence of people living on his land hundreds of years ago, new knowledge that (he later told us) enriched his life. We made the sherds *significant* for him, as they were for us. From the occurrence of these sherds—grayish-brown, the clay tempered with ground-up bits of rock, the pot surface impressed with a twined-fabric bag—we built a *chain of signification* linking the sherd traits to a style found in northeastern Montana and adjacent Alberta, Canada, in occupations dated (by radiocarbon and associated artifacts) from about AD 1300 to the nineteenth century. Historically, according to fur traders' accounts, this region was Blackfoot territory. Linking the style's range of occurrence to the historic range of the Blackfoot nation, we interpreted the sherds to have been made by Blackfoot; the fact that Blackfoot stopped making their own pots when they could obtain metal kettles from European traders, around 1830, reinforced our interpretation that the rancher's sites represented occupations earlier than the establishment of the historic fur trade in northern Montana.

Chains of signification may be much longer than that of the Blackfoot sherds example. Interpreting the Moose Mountain pattern of boulder lines required linking the alignments to astronomical phenomena, a task undertaken by our professional astronomer collaborator, and to descriptions of observations of those phenomena by societies in the historic past and in the present. Our astronomer interpreted the set of alignments to fit observation of summer solstice, both directly and by noting other star risings and settings close to that time, and in its evening. We therefore linked the site to events correlated with summer solstice, on the northern Plains before United States colonization and in other nomadic plains-dwelling societies. Our chain linked to descriptions of the big early-summer rendezvous held by northern Plains nations, events where necessary economic and social transactions could be made, so we interpreted Moose Mountain to have been a means to determine when people should travel to their important rendezvous. When we published our work at Moose Mountain, we included the astronomer's empirical data and interpretation and our references to historic and ethnographic descriptions of the early-summer rendezvous of nomadic Plains peoples—spelling out our chain of signification.

Inference to the best explanation is the principle guiding scientists. If you want to sound cool, you can use its acronym, IBE. The word that matters is "inference:" looking at data, drawing from them a reasonable explanation of how they came to be as you have observed them. More than one explanation may seem reasonable, so you test one against the other by checking the chains of signification (Are there gaps where there should be links?) and looking for exceptions and "ifs." Too many instances of "if this . . . if that," as in "If this bar that the Maya lord holds is a spaceship gear shift," weaken an explanation. What we want is a strong empirical link, for example, "The bar held by a Maya lord in this sculpture closely resembles bars placed in tombs of richly outfitted Maya identified by hieroglyphs as kings." Then we can infer that the bar held by royal Maya is a symbol of their office and power; a better explanation than one requiring "if it's a spaceship gearshift," "if extraterrestrials came to the Maya," or "if hundreds of archaeologists are dead wrong." Generally, the choice of best explanation is tougher: Is the Lord of Yaxchilán, pictured there with his bar scepter, the same king as the lord with a scepter pictured at the rival city of Calakmul? Was he a guest or a conquered king? The archaeologist grappling with these questions works with hieroglyph texts, other symbols pictured or in tombs, radiocarbon and Maya-calendar dates, even estimates of city size for Yaxchilán and Calakmul, to infer the best explanation, knowing that next season's new data may demote this explanation. IBE never promises eternal truths. It does, however, demand taking into account all data that are likely to be relevant, establishing the links between observed data and interpretive models or explanations, and showing reason to reject competing explanations.

IBE differs from a method popular in the 1970s among American archaeologists, called H-D (for "hypothetico-deductive"). H-D was used by physicists to suggest possible explanations or models, then carrying out experiments testing whether they generated predicted data. Archaeologists carrying out experiments, for example in flint-knapping to replicate ancient tools, or reconstructing buildings, can use H-D to test the feasibility of possible techniques. In this way, it was basically IBE. A fundamental difficulty for archaeologists with H-D is that the H's (the hypotheses) tended to be culture-bound—that is, what educated 1970s Euro-Americans were brought up to think. These researchers might premise—assume—that prehistoric Americans stayed in one locale and had fairly simple economies and political organization. First Nations' orally transmitted histories could be dismissed as myths. The notions that American First Nations were primitive and that their histories were fantasies were "popular knowledge" for Americans and Europeans, ideas that could be taken for granted, false and disrespectful though they are. Oral histories are, of course, difficult to verify via H-D testing.

To give an instance of the limitations that tended to undermine formal H-D interpretation, consider the hypothesis that round pit-houses in the Southwest evolved into above-ground rectangular-room apartment blocks to adapt to climate change. This hypothesis led the researcher to collect data on climate change which did, in fact, correlate loosely with the change over generations from pit-house to Pueblo. What the hypothesis did not consider were towns in an adjacent "culture area" with rectangular above-ground houses that could have been copied by the pit-house dwellers. Given that such houses, their pottery, and the agriculture of their inhabitants were outliers of the great Mexican civilizations, IBE would expect a researcher to consider an explanation that included the attraction such towns would have held to pit-house villagers. Given that pit-house villages were well-suited to Southwestern climate, the best explanation for the shift in housing type may be that the villagers imitated features of the busy towns they occasionally visited. An explanation taking in the broader social, political, and economic contexts of the pit-house-to-Pueblo change fits in with histories told by Southwestern First Nations and challenges "popular knowledge" that American Indians were primitive.

Enthusiastic proponents of H-D "hypothesis testing" claimed that they alone were scientists. They wanted to have lots of statistics and statistical formulae, as if science is only about numbers. When one such self-proclaimed scientific archaeologist was shown an obsidian blade chemically sourced to the famous Pachuca quarry north of Mexico City but excavated in the tomb of a Mississippian-period lord of a town on the Arkansas River in the United States, instead of realizing that it proved prehistoric trade between the southern United States and Mexico, he snorted, "It's only one piece. One piece isn't statistically significant!" This is like saying that Einstein had no importance because he was just one of billions of humans.

By the beginning of the twenty-first century, the notions that H-D hypothesis testing was the only scientific method and that statistics must rule were in decline. Academics following the touted theories had called themselves "processual" archaeologists, so those who rejected that routine were tagged "post-processualists." Post-processualists wanted to meld scientific procedures with greater diversity of hypotheses and interpretations. A few went out to do fieldwork with non-Western communities, calling it "ethno-archaeology" as they paid particular attention to the people's material culture and how parts of it would, and other items not, be preserved. Others sat down with American Indians or Australian Aborigines to hear what they knew of their forebears' ways of life and histories. Contemporary archaeologists, having attended schools more inclusive of cultural diversity than was common in previous centuries, may be more open to unaccustomed points of view, and more appreciative of singular finds such as a Mexican obsidian blade in Arkansas. Critical thinking recognizes that, as the philosopher C. S. Peirce put it, "surprising facts" are likely to push us to work toward inferring the best explanation.

CONTEMPORARY ARCHAEOLOGY IN THE WORLD

It is a surprising fact that archaeology is a billion-dollar business today.[1] This fact reflects the ethos that most of us espouse, that we are stewards of our planet. Obvious as that may be, from the sixteenth through the twentieth centuries political leaders encouraged deforestation, mining, and ever more powerful technology to change the earth. Francis Bacon, Lord Chancellor of England in 1618, praised mining and metallurgy as the greatest sciences because they ripped resources from "Nature's womb" and subjected them to fiery heat and hammering. Bacon's vivid language portrayed Nature as a veiled woman resisting Man's domination. An earlier (and later, counterculture) image saw Nature as a mother providing for her children, so long as they did not violently tear her open. By landing men on the moon, and propelling spacecraft to Mars and outer planets, late-twentieth-century citizens transcended earthly limits. Have we dominated Nature? Earthquakes, tsunamis and hurricanes tell us, No! On a smaller scale, we see more and more investment needed to secure basic necessities such as water, heat, and electricity. Hundreds of thousands still die from famine. Like it or not, we cannot escape the realization that our planet is a finite body. On a human-life time scale, most of what we take from the earth will not be replenished. That includes all the data from our human past.

Cultural resource management is part of our present ethos of conserving resources. We realize that conservation is vital; we pay millions of dollars to scientists researching and advising on sustaining our heritage, from soil and mineral deposits to human constructions. Heritage tourism, including eco-tourism, in turn builds on the public's consciousness that we live upon our past. Archaeology produces knowledge of that human past, in conjunction with ecologists, geologists, and other scientists placing us in the natural world.

The peculiar advantage of archaeology is its struggle to make bits of material culture tell us real history. That is why working in archaeology is a good way to understand and develop skill in critical thinking. Because it's about people and their societies, "popular knowledge" assumes "it's human nature to . . ." have chiefs rule, think time is money, support families by men's labor—premises taken from our own Western culture. Ethnographic analogies provide alternate assumptions about proper human behavior, provoking archaeologists to question pictures of the past showing simple versions of our own way of life. Artifacts as simple as sharp-edged stone flakes—quickly made, disposable knife blades—open debates over whether it is human nature to value efficiency or value patient craftsmanship, because both are amply evidenced by archaeology. Apparently egalitarian independent communities are seen in some landscapes, stupendous monuments to aristocratic rule in others. The late emergence of agriculture impresses upon us how unnatural it is to radically upset ecological systems, and evidence of collapsed agricultural regimes suggests how precarious it may be. From the long perspective of archaeology, we discover how humans have lived, and can live. The fun is in finding what no one has seen for hundreds or thousands of years, and inferring details about ancient lives from these fragments. The practical side is that our economy pays for archaeology.

You can make a living as an archaeologist, participate as a volunteer or visitor, or just sharpen your thinking skills with the real-life puzzles in archaeology. A proliferation of jobs for archaeologists in cultural resource management offers diverse opportunities. CRM companies employ business managers, public-relations and outreach people, grants writers, historical researchers, statisticians, and laboratory and field technicians, as well as dirt archaeologists. Many firms are small enough that employees can perform several roles.

State and tribal historic preservation offices oversee the gamut of sites within their jurisdictions, from Paleoindian to twentieth century.

They involve archaeologists with citizens ranging from knowledgeable avocational researchers, through community organizations and builders interested in cooperating, to occasional irate property owners sure that the Constitution gives them the right to do anything they damn well please with their land. (It doesn't.) Working with tribal cultural or historic preservation offices can be especially fascinating as the archaeologist collaborates to translate a First Nation's viewpoint and oral history into an Anglo-bureaucratic framework. Whether academic or CRM, today's archaeologists are anything but isolated.

Note

[1] Jeffrey H. Altschul, President, Statistical Research, Inc., personal communication with Alice Kehoe, November 16, 2006.

Appendix

OPPORTUNITIES AND CAREERS IN ARCHAEOLOGY

By now, you know that archaeology is an exciting and interesting field of study. Here are many opportunities to follow your interest, at the educated layperson or professional levels.

So you are not planning on becoming a professional archaeologist? You can still actively participate in archaeology. Some universities, colleges, and governmental agencies offer outreach programs in archaeology. These programs can include public lectures, or classes about a particular region or time period, or they may be field courses designed to introduce people to archaeology by participating in an actual excavation. Many professional archaeologists rely on volunteers to help with their fieldwork, and this often results in opportunities to participate in a survey, an excavation, or to work in the laboratory.

Citizens also get involved in preserving their local archaeological resources, those limited and nonrenewable windows into the past. Archaeological sites and artifacts must be protected so that we and future generations can continue to learn about the past. Consequently, public awareness, legislation, and proper management are vital to conserve these resources. At the national level, the Archaeological Conservancy was formed to rescue and preserve archaeological sites in the United States that are in danger of being destroyed. The Archaeological Conservancy raises private funds to purchase sites that would otherwise be destroyed as a result of development. The Conservancy also works to raise public awareness of archaeology in the United States, publishing a lively magazine, *American Archaeology.* As citizens, you can get involved by contacting your local archaeological and/or historical society, the Archaeological Conservancy, or the Society for American Archaeology.

Professional archaeologists are those who are paid to do archaeology for their livelihood. Professionals have a wide variety of job possibilities open to them, such as working as a field excavator, directing or assisting with research at a museum or university, or becoming a professor. What type of education must one have to become a professional archaeologist? For most jobs, a master's degree is the minimum requirement, while a doctorate is expected for an academic or senior-level research position.

The initial degree in the field is usually the four-year baccalaureate degree (a BS or BA). Many larger universities have bachelor's programs in anthropology that focus on archaeology. A handful of universities in North America now offer undergraduate degrees specifically in archaeology or archaeological studies. These programs include courses in the prehistory of various areas of the world, archaeological theory and methods courses, and analysis courses. Additional courses in physical and cultural anthropology are usually required as well. Students of archaeology should take an archaeology field-school course early on in their undergraduate studies. Archaeology field schools are actual excavations that train students in field methods. You will find out after taking a field-school course that archaeology is very labor intensive, requiring hard physical labor and a great deal of patience.

Besides anthropology and archaeology courses, undergraduate students should have a good foundation in the liberal arts from a variety of communications courses (written and oral), science courses (both natural and social sciences), humanities and fine arts courses. Students may also want to take courses that would complement archaeology training, including coursework in history, geography, geology, human anatomy, photography, and computer science. Communication skills are important, so training in public speaking, rhetoric and writing, teaching, and computer media programs are useful. An anthropology or archaeology major or minor makes a great undergraduate liberal-arts field of study, sharpening critical thinking skills and exposing students to a wide range of topics on humanity's past, present, and future.

For students wanting to become professional archaeologists, the bachelor's degree is the foundation for graduate school. There are job opportunities with a B.S./B.A. in archaeology, but most of these are at the level of "archaeological technician" (otherwise known as "shovel-bum") and are entry-level assistant positions.

Graduate school programs in anthropology/archaeology consist of masters (M.A./M.S.) and/or doctorate (Ph.D.) programs. Prospective graduate students in archaeology will need high grades and strong letters of recommendation from their undergraduate professors to get into the graduate program of their choice. The master's degree usually takes two years of study beyond the B.S./B.A. and is an entry to many jobs in contract archaeology businesses (CRM or cultural resource management). In the United States, federally funded or licensed development projects are required to take into account their impact on archaeological resources. Many states have similar laws designed to manage and protect archaeological sites. Complying with these laws requires survey work to locate archaeological sites on proposed construction projects, testing to determine site significance and eligibility for possible listing in the National Register of Historic Properties, and if evaluated as significant, modification of the project or excavation before the construction takes place.

CRM provides a wide variety of archaeology jobs. Archaeologists are hired by state and federal agencies to make certain that the agency complies with all laws related to historic preservation. In addition to government CRM positions, there are private firms that specialize in this type of archaeology, usually bidding on archaeological research projects that must be done before a development project can proceed. CRM firms not only hire M.A./M.S. archaeologists as supervisors, they also hire undergraduates and B.S./B.A. holders as field-crew workers for surveys and excavations. CRM archaeology now accounts for the vast majority of archaeological field projects conducted in the United States and Canada. The end product of CRM archaeology is usually a written report summarizing the fieldwork and analysis of the archaeological materials recovered during the project. CRM has added greatly to our understanding of the past, because many of these projects would not have existed if it were not for state and federal historic preservation laws requiring archaeological investigations.

Museums hire archaeologists for both research and educational programs. Museum archaeologists may work on developing an interpretive display for the public or behind the scenes, managing archaeological collections and archives. Collection managers oversee inventorying, cataloguing, preservation, and archival storage of archaeological materials. Since archaeological materials are nonrenewable resources, it is important that they be stored in controlled environments to ensure safe, long-term storage. Museums regularly allow archaeologists from outside institutions to work with their collections. Archaeological methods of investigation are constantly improving and evolving, encouraging reanalysis of existing collections using more modern techniques. Properly stored and catalogued archaeological collections are priceless sources of information for future researchers.

Some larger museums also employ archaeologists to conduct fieldwork to enhance their archaeological collections. Archaeologists working in this capacity may oversee excavations during the warmer months while spending their winters overseeing the processing and analysis of the materials recovered from the summer excavations.

Universities and colleges employ archaeologists as both teaching professors and researchers. Although it possible to find a part-time archaeology teaching job at a college if you have a master's degree, full-time positions usually require the Ph.D. All professors are expected to teach and to be involved in their fields in terms of research and service. Smaller universities and liberal arts colleges generally have heavier teaching loads, and an archaeologist may be required to teach classes in the other subfields of anthropology. Teaching in this environment can be highly rewarding by facilitating professorial interaction with undergraduate students in smaller classroom settings than can be found at the larger research universities. Even at small colleges, faculty will spend their summers in the field, working on excavations and teaching undergraduates the basics of field archaeology.

Large research universities with graduate programs in anthropology and archaeology strongly encourage their faculty to publish their research on a regular basis and to seek out external grant funding to support their projects. Graduate students working on advanced degrees take a specialized upper-level curriculum and work on their own research. In this environment, professors specialize in a particular area of archaeology and offer courses related to their research. These professors supervise their graduate students' research by overseeing their data collection, analyses, and report writing. Teaching and conducting research at a large university with a graduate program in archaeology can be challenging and exciting. Students in these programs become the next generation of archaeologists working in field, classroom, and museums.

Professional archaeology organizations operate throughout the United States and Canada. The largest is the Society for American Archaeology (SAA). Most professional archaeologists practicing in North America belong to the SAA, and membership is also available at a reduced rate for students of archaeology and avocationals. SAA's professional journal, *American Antiquity*, presents detailed material on current methods, theories, and discoveries. All articles submitted for publication are peer-reviewed by other professionals to make certain they adhere to scientific methods and are thoroughly researched. SAA annually holds national conferences for archaeologists to present their recent research, and it supports public awareness and outreach for archaeology by working with teachers, avocational archaeologists, and the government. The Archaeological Institute of America (AIA) parallels SAA in bringing together interested public and professionals. AIA focuses internationally, especially the archaeology of the Mediterranean—Greece, Rome, and the Near and Middle East. Through its dozens of local chapters appealing to the general public, AIA brings audiences famous archaeologists lecturing on newsworthy sites; its popular-style magazine *Archaeology* caters to readers wanting to know more about such finds. In addition to SAA and AIA, there are regional, state, and local organizations. Many allow members of the general public and students who are interested in archaeology to join, participate in meetings, and receive their own regional journal. Checking with your local college's archaeologist will put you in touch with quality programs at whatever level interests you.

ARCHAEOLOGY-RELATED WEB SITES

The Society for American Archaeology—http://www.saa.org
Archaeological Institute of America—www.archaeological.org
Society for Historical Archaeology—www.sha.org
The Archaeological Conservancy—
 www.americanarchaeology.com/aaabout
World Archaeological Congress—www.worldarchaeologicalcongress.org
Institute for Nautical Archaeology—nautarch.tamu.edu
Advisory Council on Underwater Archaeology—www. acuaonline.org

CURRENT AND PROPOSED NORTH AMERICAN WORLD HERITAGE SITES

UNESCO recognizes these archaeologically researched World Heritage Sites in the United States:

- Cahokia (Illinois)
- Chaco (New Mexico)
- Mesa Verde (Colorado)
- Pueblo de Taos, New Mexico (still a living community)

Other U. S. archaeological sites that have been proposed as world-class heritage include:

- Blackwater Draw (Paleoindian, in New Mexico)
- Cape Krusenstern Archaeological District (Alaska)
- Casa Grande and other Hohokam (Arizona)
- Effigy mound sites (Wisconsin and Iowa)
- Jamestown (first successful English colony) (Virginia)
- Mound City and Newark Earthworks (Hopewell culture, in Ohio)
- Moundville (Mississippian culture, in Alabama)
- Ocmulgee (Georgia)

- Ozette (Washington)
- Pecos Pueblo (New Mexico)
- Pinson Mounds (Tennessee)
- Poverty Point (Louisiana)
- Pu'uhonua O Honaunau (Hawaii)
- St. Augustine (Spanish-founded colony, in Florida)
- Serpent Mound (Ohio)

Among Canadian World Heritage sites are L'Anse aux Meadows (Newfoundland), an AD 1000 Viking Norse settlement; and Head-Smashed-In Buffalo Jump (Alberta), both with substantial interpretive centers. Writing-on-Stone (Alberta), featuring a wealth of Plains Indian rock art along a beautiful valley, is a provincial park proposed for World Heritage listing. Mexico's great ancient cities designated as World Heritage sites include Teotihuacán, Palenque, and Monte Albán.

Published Sources

Chapter 1

Bahn, Paul G. 1996. *Cambridge Illustrated History: Archaeology*. Cambridge: Cambridge University Press.

Piggott, Stuart 1981. Summary and Conclusions. In Glyn Daniel (ed.), *Towards a History of Archaeology*, pp. 186–189. London and New York: Thames and Hudson.

Scarre, Chris (ed.). 2005. *The Human Past: World Prehistory and the Development of Human Societies*. London and New York: Thames and Hudson. (Massive, detailed, well-illustrated, and readable, with many boxes highlighting special finds and controversies.)

Chapter 2

Bass, George F. (ed.). 2005. *Beneath the Seven Seas: Adventures with the Institute of Nautical Archaeology* London and New York: Thames and Hudson.

Green, Jeremy. 2004. *Maritime Archaeology: A Technical Handbook*. Amsterdam: Elsevier Academic Press.

Orser, Charles E., Jr. 2002. *Encyclopedia of Historical Archaeology*. London and New York: Routledge.

Orser, Charles E., Jr. 2004. *Historical Archaeology*. Upper Saddle River, NJ: Pearson Prentice-Hall.

Orser, Charles E., Jr., and Brian M. Fagan. 1995. *Historical Archaeology*. New York: HarperCollins.

Renfrew, Colin, and Paul Bahn. 2004. *Archaeology: Theories, Methods, and Practice* (4th ed.). London and New York: Thames and Hudson. (Check for frequent revisions/new editions.)

Yamin, Rebecca, and Karen Bescherer Metheny. 1996. *Landscape Archaeology: Reading and Interpreting the American Historical Landscape*. Knoxville: University of Tennessee Press.

Chapter 3

Bahn, Paul, and Jean Vertut. 2002. *Journey through the Ice Age*. Berkeley: University of California Press.
Chippindale, Christopher. 2004. *Stonehenge Complete* (rev. ed.). London and New York: Thames and Hudson.
Evans, Susan Toby. 2004. *Ancient Mexico and Central America: Archaeology and Culture History*. London and New York: Thames and Hudson. (on Maya.)
Kehoe, Alice Beck. 2002. *America before the European Invasions*. London: Longman/Pearson Education.
Kennedy, Roger G. 1994. *Hidden Cities: The Discovery and Loss of Ancient North America*. New York: Free Press (in paperback, Penguin). (on Cahokia.)
Lister, Florence. 2004. *Troweling through Time: The First Century of Mesa Verde Archaeology*. Albuquerque: University of New Mexico Press.
Pauketat, Timothy R. 2004. *Ancient Cahokia and the Mississippians*. Cambridge: Cambridge University Press.
Reeves, Nicholas. 1990. *The Complete Tutankhamun*. London and New York: Thames and Hudson. (In this publisher's series, see also Mark Lehner, 1997, *The Complete Pyramids*.)
Vernus, Pascal, and Jean Yoyotte. 2003. *The Book of the Pharaohs*. Translated by David Lorton. Ithaca: Cornell University Press.

Chapter 4

Baxter, Jane Eva. 2005. Gendered Perceptions of Archaeology. *SAA Archaeological Record* 5(4):7–9.

Chapter 5

Birmingham, Robert A. and Leslie E. Eisenberg. 2000. *Indian Mounds of Wisconsin*. Madison: The University of Wisconsin Press.
Birmingham, Robert A., Carol I. Mason, and James B. Stoltman (eds.). 1997. Wisconsin Archaeology. *The Wisconsin Archeologist* 78(1/2).
Mason, Ronald J. 1981. *Great Lakes Archaeology*. New York: Academic Press.
Martin, Susan R.1999. *Wonderful Power: The Story of Ancient Copper Working in the Lake Superior Basin*. Detroit: Wayne State University Press.
Pleger, Thomas C. 2000. Old Copper and Red Ocher Social Complexity. *Midcontinental Journal of Archaeology*, 25(2):169–190.
Pleger, Thomas C. 2001. New Dates for the Oconto Old Copper Culture Cemetery. In T. C. Pleger, Thomas C., R. A. Birmingham, and C. I. Mason (eds.), Papers in Honor of Carol I. Mason. *The Wisconsin Archeologist* 82(1 & 2):87–100.
Theler, James L., and Robert F. Boszhardt. 2003. *Twelve Millennia: Archaeology of the Upper Mississippi River Valley*. Iowa City: University of Iowa Press.

Chapter 6

Kehoe, Alice Beck. 1998. *The Land of Prehistory: A Critical History of American Archaeology*. New York: Routledge.
Kehoe, Alice Beck (in press). *Controversies in Archaeology*. Walnut Creek, CA: Left Coast Press (estimated 2007 publication date).
Kelley, Jane H., and Marsha P. Hanen. 1988. *Archaeology and the Methodology of Science*. Albuquerque: University of New Mexico Press.

Chapter 7

King, Thomas F. 2003. *Places That Count: Traditional Cultural Properties in Cultural Resource Management*. Walnut Creek, CA: AltaMira.

Zimmerman, Larry J., Karen D. Vitelli, and Julie Hollowell-Zimmer (eds.). 2003. *Ethical Issues in Archaeology*. Walnut Creek, CA: AltaMira.

Chapter 8

Merchant, Carolyn. 1980. *The Death of Nature*. San Francisco: Harper and Row.

Kehoe, Alice B., and Thomas F. Kehoe, 1979. *Solstice-Aligned Boulder Configurations in Saskatchewan*. Ottawa: Canadian Ethnology Service Paper No. 48, Mercury Series, National Museum of Man.

Index